Adventure
Riding Techniques

First published in March 2009
Reprinted April 2010

A catalogue record for this book is available from the British Library

ISBN 978 1 84425 572 6

Library of Congress catalog card no 2008939600

Published by Haynes Publishing,
Sparkford, Yeovil, Somerset BA22 7JJ, UK
Tel: +44 1963 442030 Fax: +44 1963 440001
E-mail: sales@haynes.co.uk
Website: www.haynes.co.uk

Haynes North America Inc.,
861 Lawrence Drive, Newbury Park,
California 91320, USA

Printed and bound in the USA

📷 BMW Motorrad

Dedication
Robert Wicks

For Rog

Greg Baker

To my wife Sue for her unstinting support and enthusiasm during the writing of this book, and for my Dad who would have been proud to see the finished work.

And to Robert Wicks, for his vision, drive, and (above all) his friendship – long may it continue; and Austin Vince for his unforgettable quote that *'everyone should eventually drink from the goblet of real adventure motorcycling, because it is good.'*

Acknowledgements
The authors would like to thank the following people for their support and expertise:

Nik Boseley, Danny Burroughs, Andy Dukes, Steve Eilertsen, Johan Engelbrecht, Scott Grimsdall, Mark Hodson, Jim Hyde, Mark Ingleby, Tony Jakeman, Adam Lewis, Jonathan Lloyd, Kylie Maebus, Joe Pichler, Nick Plumb, Lois Pryce, Julia Sanders, Kevin Sanders, Shaun Sisterson, Chris Smith, Barry Urand, Austin Vince, Waldo van der Waal, Juergen Weisz, and Rodney Womack.

They would also like to extend special thanks to:

Simon Pavey – for his time, enthusiasm and commitment to this project. Not only is he an outstanding rider, but also a great teacher, and a friend whose love of off-road motorcycling is evident in everything he does.

The team at Biking Vikings – Eythor Orlygsson, Ingolfur Stefansson, Njall Gunnlaugsson, Hjortur L. Jonsson, Thorgeir Olason, and Thorvaldur Orn Kristmundsson for their time and dedication during a wonderful week in Iceland where we gathered the vast majority of material for this book.

Mark Hughes – Editorial Director at Haynes Publishing, for his belief in the project from the start and support throughout the editorial process.

Lee Parsons – Senior Designer at Haynes Publishing, for the outstanding design and interpretation of the subject matter.

Adventure
Riding Techniques

The essential guide to all the skills you need for off-road adventure riding

Robert Wicks & Greg Baker
Foreword by **Simon Pavey**

Contents

BMW Motorrad

I'm always reminded of the image in Rob's first book, *Adventure Motorcycling*, of the four folk who have just come off the trail and are so glad to see the tarmac they're kissing it! I guess I see things differently.

As a teenager growing up in Australia, every weekend was an off-road adventure. A posse of us would set out from my parents' house, sneaking through the back suburban streets as quickly as we could, and then we were into the sand dunes. The day was spent chasing our way to the far end of the peninsula on brilliant trails before making a run to the petrol station for enough 'liquid gold' to make it back home.

When I wasn't out riding, I was reading about it and would often find myself captivated by media coverage of some of the world's exotic rallies: the Incas Rally in Peru; the Dakar Rally, and the Roof of Africa.

In 1988 I raced in the Rally des Cagous on the Pacific island of New Caledonia. This was a significant event for many reasons – not only does still it bring back some of my fondest racing memories, but it is also where I met my wife, Linley, and it was from here that we decided to move to Europe for the rallying.

Twenty years later, seven Dakar Rallies, the Roof of Africa, and numerous other overland competitions under my belt, and I still have the same bug, only now it's with a new twist. These days, in between competing, my real passion is sharing my love of off-road riding with others and this is where Off Road Skills was born.

The growth in the school over the past few years is indicative of the popularity of adventure motorcycling, but for many people off-road riding is not something they might consider, still going far but sticking instead to the tarmac. The thought of having to deal with a heavy adventure bike over unpredictable terrain is a real deterrent for some, but I believe it is only once you are off the beaten track and truly riding off-road that you will discover just what adventure motorcycling can do for the soul.

It's fair to say that out on the trail, the situations you are likely to face will be more challenging than normal road riding, but if you can grasp and apply the two most important aspects – to always maintain maximum control of your bike and at the same time to try and minimise levels of fatigue – then there is no reason why you shouldn't be out there enjoying yourself.

When Rob and Greg asked for my help with this new book about adventure riding techniques it fitted straight in with my passion, and it's what I teach people everyday at the school in Wales. I genuinely hope it inspires you to take to the dirt. Take in the key techniques on the pages that follow, enjoy the inspirational images and ride, ride, ride.

Just no more kissing the tarmac, OK!

Simon Pavey
March 2009

Simon Pavey on his way to completing the 2009 Dakar Rally in Argentina and Chile
📷 Maindru Photo

ORS
Off Road Skills

Introduction

Ted Simon is quoted as saying that he comes from the group of motorcyclists who would rather go far than fast. Going far – or 'adventure motorcycling' as we prefer to call it – is the fusion of the joy of motorcycling and the thrill of exploration, and it brings what once we regarded as distant horizons within our grasp. It's neither sport nor pastime, but encompasses an ethos of discovery, both of the world and of the self.

Adventure motorcycling requires a variety of skills, and presents challenges that may at first seem daunting to many. Aside from the financial and time commitments, and the necessary planning and border-crossing paperwork, you will be riding over terrain and in weather that you are unfamiliar with, and you will need to be able to deal with whatever mechanical problems arise en route. But, above all, and really the reason why this book was written, is riding technique. You may think you already know how to ride a motorcycle, but very few people realise that, through just a few simple adjustments to their riding style, and being aware of some key things, the entire experience of going far can be made more rewarding, less tiring, and safer. Many forget that a motorcycle is a rider-active vehicle, meaning that you have to move your body around to control the bike. Not moving, or moving the wrong way, can ruin traction, upset the suspension, and quickly tire you out. The higher the level of control you have over the bike, the less fatigued you are likely to feel.

As veteran adventure riding instructor, Jim Hyde, says: 'When you condense the important aspects of adventure riding, it comes down to balance and control. You can't emphasise that enough. Keep your bike upright and in line, and even the heaviest machine will feel light and nimble. If you lose the balance, the bike instantly becomes heavy. The trick is getting the bike back in balance quickly. Many riders actually ride "out of balance" and wonder why they feel so tired after a day's ride.'

Adventure Riding Techniques, based on our own many miles of experience and consultations with several leading experts, is the definitive guide that will teach you all you need to know about adventure bike basics, riding positions and techniques, crossing different types of terrain, and strategies for survival; and it will give you the confidence to undertake a long-distance ride.

Whether you are a first-time adventurer looking to develop your skills, or a more experienced rider wanting to employ more specialist techniques, it will help you to get the best out of both yourself and your motorcycle in all circumstances.

Equipped with this information you too can join the group that like to go far.

We hope you enjoy the read.

Robert Wicks and Greg Baker
March 2009

Chapter 1
Adventure motorcycling

📷 Joe Pichler

I t is unlikely that New Yorker Carl Stevens Clancy, when he circumnavigated the globe on his four-cylinder Henderson in 1913, imagined the profound effect he would have on long-distance motorcycling.

Stevens, whose world tour took him through 16 countries and four continents in just eight months, and a raft of other pioneers such as Robert Edison Fulton and Stanley Glanfield, laid the foundations for what we know today as adventure motorcycling by showing what could be achieved with some fairly elementary machinery.

To attempt an expedition such as that of Fulton or Glanfield today would be an achievement in its own right, but to have succeeded in the 1920s and 1930s when motorcycles were considerably less reliable, roads – where they existed – were often badly maintained, spares were almost non-existent, and fuel supplies were at best sporadic, is nothing short of an achievement of epic proportions.

More recently, the likes of Ted Simon, Helge Pedersen, Bernd Tesch, Danny Liska, Ed Culberson, Grant Johnson, and Chris Scott have all had a significant impact on adventure motorcycling, while the exploits of Ewan McGregor and Charley Boorman's 'Long Way Round' and 'Long Way Down' expeditions in the last few years have added a new dimension and propelled the notion of a serious overland trip into more homes than ever before.

Scott describes overland travel as 'a challenging journey into the wilderness or a significantly strange country'. He views the motorcycle as a tool with which 'to escape from the mundane and predictable'. Adventure motorcycling, or 'overlanding', has enjoyed a huge growth in popularity over the last decade, and what once was the privilege of wealthy eccentrics has now become accessible to many of us. Whilst some motorcycle manufacturers have taken tentative steps and produced machines with an adventure façade, others have fully embraced this unique sector, making 'continent-conquering' machines genuinely capable of global off-road travel.

The modern adventure motorcycle comes in a variety of guises, from the modified enduro dirt-bike to a specifically designed behemoth, but they all share an ability to go to places

Touratech

that are otherwise inaccessible to normal mainstream travellers. Serious overlanders tend to be a breed apart, fiercely protecting the mystique of their chosen vocation, but with a little vision and the desire to take that extra step, the whole world starts to open out in front of us all.

In his book *Riding the World*, motorcycle journalist Gregory Frazier says adventure motorcycling 'allows people to escape daily routines, to seek answers to life's questions and to challenge themselves'. It is this quest to get away from it all, to escape the routines and the monotony of work, and to accept the challenge of riding into the unknown that makes adventure motorcycling such a fascinating subject.

Escaping, and riding into uncharted territory naturally comes with certain risks, and the more proficient you are in terms of technical skill and an understanding of how best to control your motorcycle under varying conditions, the more manageable those risks become and the more enjoyable the overall experience. ■

Choosing an adventure motorcycle

Aspiring adventure riders are spoilt for choice today. Of all the different categories of motorcycles available, the adventure segment of the market has arguably seen the most significant levels of growth, with nearly every major manufacturer launching a new machine that they claim will see you round the world. Some can rightly make this claim, others not.

Big trail bike models such as the KTM 990 Adventure and BMW R1200GS Adventure are both well equipped for all terrain use, and can comfortably cope with cross-continental expeditions with potentially very little modification to the machine which initially rolls off the showroom floor. At the same time, other manufacturers have opted for models which exhibit 'adventure' qualities, but underneath the skin are really road bikes with an adventure-orientated façade, and this should always be borne in mind when making a purchasing decision.

Much of this growth in the market can be attributed to changing lifestyles and preferences as consumers opt for a motorcycle fully capable of allowing them to escape the confines of modern living for a weekend, a week, a year, or more.

The majority of machines in the sector tend to have large capacity engines (600–1,200cc) intended for operating more than comfortably as a road tourer, but equally adept on gravel tracks or even rougher terrain. For all their capacity and load-carrying ability, the biggest downside is weight, which can make them tough to handle in extreme conditions. The added weight means your technique needs to be at a good level, as does your fitness, since manoeuvring a big trail bike with luggage across tough terrain can be very demanding, and increased levels of fatigue are something you need to avoid at all costs. A smaller, lighter, and more nimble off-road enduro style machine (300–600cc) is best suited to dealing with arduous terrain, but this too can be

↑ BMW's R1200GS Adventure – it will certainly see you round the world
📷 MCN

↑ Just another day in the office for this BMW rider
📷 BMW Motorrad

a compromise as your on-road ability is often reduced, the load carrying capacity is generally less, as is the bike's range unless fitted with a long-range fuel tank.

Before making any commitment, be sure to ask yourself: 'How good is my technique?' and 'How fit will I be when I embark on the adventure?' as these are critical elements in your decision. Once this is clear, you then need to consider the following specifics about individual bikes:

Price – Remember that a brand-new, high-end, all-conquering adventure bike may look like the best choice from the images of remote locations in the sales literature, but this is likely to come at a significant cost and will have a serious knock-on effect on what you are charged for your carnet (customs permit), which in turn can put a large dent in your overall budget. Explore second-hand options thoroughly, but be sure you are getting value for money and a machine that is in good condition and capable of the trip.

Timing and availability – The sooner you get your bike the better. As an experienced motorcyclist you will already have a fair idea of how you want to customise it, and as a novice you will need as much time with your new best friend as possible. Furthermore, orders for certain parts you might want may take time to be fulfilled by aftermarket suppliers.

Range and consumption – Consider the distances you will need to travel between refuelling points and make sure the bike's range is suitable. Fuel consumption is also important – a big 1,000cc engine, for example, can be a thirsty beast, particularly when working hard in the desert. Remember that more fuel means more weight.

Load-carrying ability – Assess how much you need to carry and how the bike will cope with the load. Adding weight impacts on manoeuvrability, and can increase rider fatigue, particularly over rough terrain.

Terrain – Research and understand the terrain you are going to be covering – some bikes are more suited to certain types of terrain than others.

Spares and reliability – Ideally, you want to choose a machine with a proven track record, and one which is likely to have readily-available spares which you can either buy on the road or source with relative ease from home.

Mechanical knowledge – Appreciate that you will need a level of mechanical competence to deal with technical issues that will arise from time to time. At the very least, you should know how to carry out a basic service on the machine.

Handling and weight – If possible, before purchasing try to ride a fully-laden machine to ascertain what you are in for. A big 1,000cc off-road bike with fully-loaded panniers and some additional gear can easily weigh in excess of 660lb (300kg).

Seat height – Ensure that the seat height allows you to reach the ground comfortably with at least one foot flat on the road surface. This does not sound that important, but it can dramatically affect your technique when riding at slow speeds, in traffic, on uneven road surfaces, or in confined places.

Be sure to research and test ride a range of alternatives before making your final decision. There is no 'perfect' overland bike because what's good off-road isn't necessarily good on-road, so choose the bike that is the best compromise for you and the trip.

⬇ **That is what I call escaping the daily routine**
📷 Carlos Azevado

⬆ **Almost any bike can be equipped to 'go far'**
📷 Metal Mule

Adventure bike basics

Technical considerations

Adventure motorcycles are beasts of a very different nature from their road-going counterparts. To meet the greater demands made of them, and to withstand the rigours of off-road touring, more robust (and heavier) materials are required, and a greater number of purpose-designed components have to be fitted, including a high-output alternator to cope with additional electrical accessories. Extra protection must be provided for vulnerable components, and enhanced cooling is often needed to cope with the extra heat generated by the engine under load. These and many other factors have steered the design process of the modern overland motorcycle. That said, you do not need to have the latest, most expensive bike, but it must be set up properly, because if it isn't, both your riding technique and safety can be compromised.

Controls

Clever use of your controls – the throttle, brakes, and clutch – makes all the difference to adventure riding. Can you ride around more slowly than first gear allows by slipping the clutch? Can you do it with very little throttle and not stall the bike? Can you apply the brakes and come to a complete stop, balanced and without putting a foot down? Then, can you use the controls to snap back into balance and ride off and feel comfortable at speed? When going off-road, being in total control is crucial.

The following list is not exhaustive but should give you an idea of the most relevant issues:

■ You first need to ensure that the handlebars are correctly positioned. When viewed from the side, the line of the handlebars should follow the line of the forks.
■ Control levers need to be correctly adjusted in terms of angle and reach of your fingers, and at an angle on the handlebars that is comfortable both in the seated and the attack riding positions.
■ Leave the control lever clamps slightly loose on the bars so that in the case of a spill they will turn on the bar rather than break.
■ Foot controls should be adjusted so that your boot toe is underneath the lever, preventing inadvertent gear changes or braking.
■ The handlebars should be a little wider than your shoulders and should not be bent. Narrow handlebars tend to cause instability of the front end. Having wide bars that are in line with your forks makes it easier to use the 'elbows up' riding style advocated throughout this book.
■ You should be able to pull your clutch and brake levers in about 5–10mm before they start working.
■ Consider lock-wiring their grips to avoid them slipping during a ride.
■ The rear brake should be adjusted to work when it has been pressed down 1cm.
■ The angle and size of your foot pegs are vital to riding well, so consider replacing existing parts with larger variations.

→ **Yamaha's new Tenere offers a good balance between load carrying ability, weight, style and performance**
📷 Yamaha

← **Adjust sag using the rear spring preload to maximise suspension travel**
📷 Greg Baker

↓ **Adjust the damping for the best ride on rough terrain**
📷 Greg Baker

Suspension and ride height

A modern adventure bike's suspension will usually be sophisticated enough to deal with most circumstances. However, it will usually be set up for the average rider under average conditions. Additional loads on the bike and extreme terrain might require a specific adjustment of the suspension settings to get the best out of the bike.

Altering the spring pre-load on your motorcycle's suspension changes the way it behaves under load. By applying more pre-load to the spring more weight is required to compress it. Similarly, reducing pre-load reduces the weight required to compress the spring. In real terms this translates to adjusting the spring's tension to give the best compromise between suspension performance and rider comfort. A large adventure bike isn't going to have a huge range of suspension adjustment, but you can get the best out of it by using pre-load effectively. The

basic settings will generally be more than adequate for an average rider's day-to-day use, but a heavier rider together with another 50kg of luggage will compress the suspension far more than a light rider and a day-pack.

It is impossible to give exact settings as every rider's requirements are different, but the main objective should be to ensure that the bike remains manageable and comfortable to ride. When adjusting suspension, make only small changes, and change only one thing at a time. Like this you will always know how each adjustment affects the bike. As you will be carrying more luggage you will probably need to increase your pre-load to compensate for the additional weight on board. Check your motorcycle's handbook as it may give guidance for the adjustment required, but in general terms active sag (that is to say suspension compression with rider and load aboard) should be around one third of the total free

↓ **You'll need to be sure your suspension is in good order if you're planning to ride like this**
📷 Thorvaldur Orn Kristmundsson

suspension travel. Using the bike's headlamp alignment can give you a good baseline to work from. Sit on the unloaded bike and shine the headlamp on a wall 10–15 feet away from you. Make a note of the height of the beam on the wall. Load the bike with an approximation of the luggage you will be carrying and do the same again. You'll probably find that the second measurement is higher than the first as the additional weight carried is compressing the rear spring more. This being the case, increase the rear suspension pre-load until the beam height with the bike loaded and rider aboard is the same as the previous unloaded beam height. By increasing the pre-load you are effectively restoring ride height which maintains the bike's level attitude on the road. Bear in mind, however, that your objective should always be to maintain stability and manageability at all times.

Compression and rebound damping are the fine adjustments that affect the quality, or so-called 'plushness' of the ride by controlling the speed at which the suspension reacts to bumps in the road. Too much compression damping and the ride will be harsh and unforgiving, too little and the suspension will 'top out' or reach the full extent of its travel too easily. Too much rebound damping will slow the suspension's return rate, restricting the amount of travel for the next bump, too little and the spring will extend too quickly and can kick the wheel off the ground, vastly reducing grip. The ideal starting point is the manufacturer's recommended setting. Set the suspension to these figures and go for a ride. If you feel the need to adjust the settings, then do so, but only after altering just one thing at a time. This way you'll be able to see and feel the effect of the changes you make, and will know what to change back if it has an adverse effect.

With the motorcycle properly adjusted, you'll find not only that the ride quality improves, but that the bike will handle a lot better both on-road and off-road, giving you the level of control you need.

Enduro front tyre **Intermediate rear tyre**

Tyres

A motorcycle's tyres are the crucial interface between the rider and the road, providing feedback on the condition of the road surface itself, and how the bike is performing in terms of traction and braking. Also, a fact easily overlooked, is that an adventure bike tyre's contact patch is probably going to be a lot smaller than that of a conventional tyre – probably close to a third in reality. When the additional weight of the bike is taken into account, it's quite remarkable how much work the tyres do in controlling braking and acceleration stability.

Tyre combinations

There are two inescapable factors to consider about motorcycle tyres: Rears always wear faster than fronts, and intermediate road tyres will last longer than knobbly enduro tyres. Typical wear rates will be 2,000–3,000 miles (3,000–5,000km) from an enduro rear tyre, 3,000–5,000 miles (5,000–8,000km) from a front, and intermediate tyres will give between 3,800–5,000 miles (6,000–8,000km) from a rear and anything up to about 6,500 miles (10,000km) from a front. A growing trend amongst long-distance overlanders is to use a combination of an intermediate tyre, such as a Michelin Anakee 2, on the rear wheel and an enduro tyre, such as a Michelin T63, fitted to the front. The nature of an intermediate tyre makes a good compromise between off-road grip and tyre life, giving about twice the mileage of an enduro tyre, so both tyres will give between 3,000–5,000 miles (5,000–8,000km). This is an ideal situation, as you end up replacing both tyres at the same time rather than one front for every two rears in the usual 2:1 rear/front ratio. This effectively means that you don't have to carry a second rear tyre if your journey is around 3,000–3,800 miles (5,000–6,000km). Consult the manufacturer in case of any doubt.

Tyre Pressures

Running tyre pressures too low means you run the risk of impact punctures. If the pressures are too high, your rear wheel will spin and not get traction. A good compromise pressure is 15–20psi, but if you feel that conditions demand it, and you can readily re-inflate the tyre, pressures can be reduced by 5psi.

↑**Making the right tyre choice is essential and depends largely on the terrain you plan to cross**
📷 Waldo van der Waal

Chassis

The loading and stresses that an adventure bike is likely to experience are very different from those a road bike encounters. Consequently its chassis is upgraded and strengthened by using extra bracing and heavy-duty materials. The most highly stressed areas are around the steering head, the rear suspension mount, the rear sub-frame, and the engine mountings. As the chassis is not a 'moving part' as such, maintenance is largely limited to visual inspection.

When washing or cleaning the bike, attention should be given to the areas mentioned above, looking for obvious things like, for example, cracks in a gusset or along a weld. More subtle signs could be traces of rust appearing along a weld line, which could suggest that a crack in the chassis has occurred, damaged the paint finish, and allowed corrosion to start. If additional webs or gussets have been welded to the frame, these should be checked for signs of buckling or warping which might suggest that the bike has suffered an impact or shock whilst loaded.

Without doubt, the most vulnerable part of any modular chassis will be the rear sub-frame, as this

component has to support the rider as well as luggage, and possibly a passenger too. If you have difficulty in aligning and mounting panniers, for example, the sub-frame may be bent. More obvious will be cracking or, in the worst case, a complete fracture. All frame bolts and engine-mounting bolts should be regularly checked for tightness, and any found to be loose re-torqued to the specified value. If you have a critical fastener that consistently loosens, then consider using a thread-locking compound to prevent further loosening.

Tools

It is important to travel light, so don't weigh yourself down by taking tools you'll never use. Take the tools that fit the fasteners on your bike, leave the others at home. If the fittings on your bike are, for example, 8, 10, 12, 13, 15 and 17mm, then only take those sized sockets and spanners. Do likewise with Allen keys or Torx drivers. Use the smallest tool you can that will do the job – for most tasks on a motorcycle a reasonable quality ³⁄₈in drive set will be more than adequate, and with an extension bar will be capable of applying very high torque. If you need greater leverage for certain nuts, then take a short length of steel tube and an adaptor to use for ½in sockets.

Other essential tool kit items include:

Mole grips – These are incredibly versatile and can be used to perform a multitude of tasks. Available in a variety of sizes, a 6in wrench is probably the most useful without being too big.

Chain tool and spare links – The American Motion-Pro brand has a breaking and riveting set which is light and very functional.

Mini compressor – A 12v compressor, stripped of its plastic body, is remarkably small and very useful.

Tyre levers and puncture repair kit – Tyre changing is an art, but can be mastered with practice. Use three 12in tyre irons. Don't rely on a small retail puncture kit if you anticipate a lot of punctures, better to buy patches and solution in bulk packs. Take a couple of spare tubes, remembering that front tubes will generally fit rear wheels, but not the other way round.

Zip ties and duct tape – These are universally useful items, but rather than taking a large roll of tape, wrap a couple of metres round something else to save space, and a handful of zip ties can be slipped into a tiny space in your tool bag.

Insulating tape – Whilst used principally for electrical purposes, this tape can also be a good stand-in for luggage strapping, wound dressing, and any other job that duct tape is too big for.

Screwdrivers – One general purpose cross-head screwdriver, one general purpose flat-head screwdriver, and one small electrical screwdriver that can double as a pick or probe.

Fast-setting epoxy – Epoxy resin, such as J-B Weld, can be used to plug holes in crankcases and fix bodywork.

Impact tools – A small hammer and punch.

Small electrical multi-meter – A simple voltage/ continuity tester.

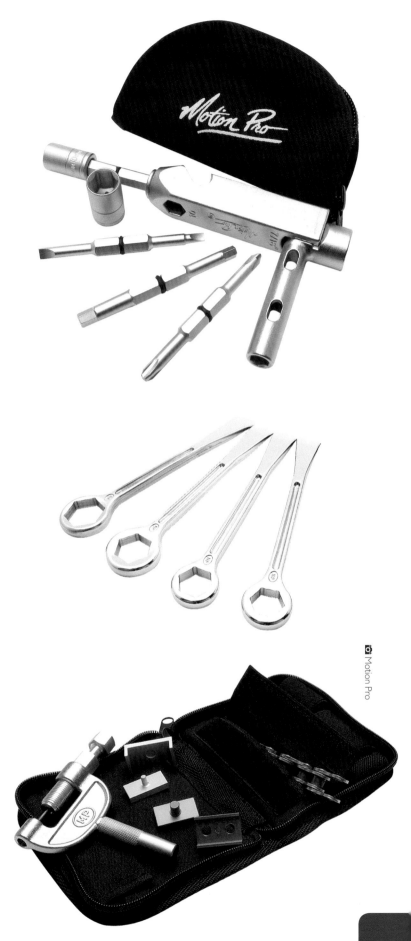

Motion Pro

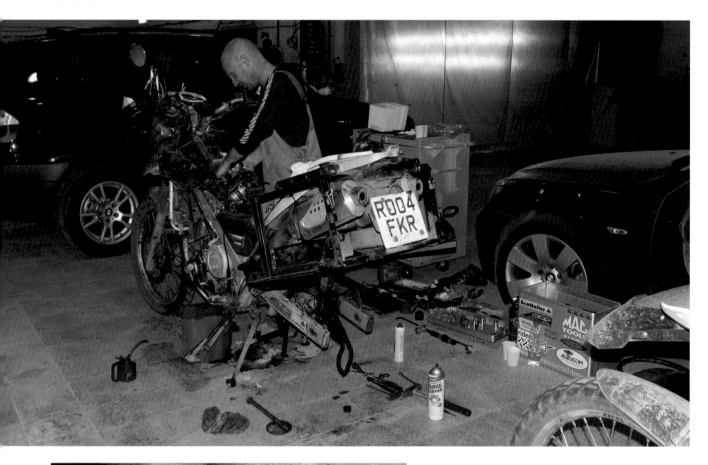

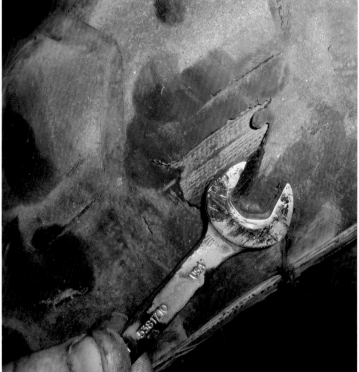

Maintenance

Modern manufacturing technology and sophisticated engine management and fuel delivery systems, coupled with regular maintenance, have all but eradicated total engine failure. However, keeping a regular check on your motorcycle is essential given the arduous nature of an adventure ride and the stresses it will place on the engine, chassis, wheels, tyres, and other components. The better condition the motorcycle is in, the better it will handle, and ultimately this will give you better control over the machine.

A regular check on oil and coolant levels not only ensures that continued protection is provided, but can also indicate a problem that might be waiting in the wings. For example, unusual rates of oil consumption could indicate worn piston rings or a failed valve stem oil seal. Falling coolant levels obviously indicates a leak somewhere. Exhaust smoke can also help diagnose problems – a continuous blue haze suggests worn rings, a puff of smoke on start-up indicates worn valve stem seals, white sweet-smelling smoke indicates coolant in the cylinder head, and possibly a blown head gasket.

Fix the seal before it lets go completely and leaves you stranded in the middle of nowhere.

Tyres should be checked visually every ride, looking for obvious signs of deflation or damage. Symptoms of damage will be the same for both tubed and tubeless tyres, and will most likely be seen as cuts or bulges in the tyre's sidewall, or missing tread blocks. Sidewall damage should be taken seriously as the weakness could rupture, causing an instant deflation. Missing tread blocks don't present such an immediate risk, but the tyre itself will be very vulnerable to punctures as the remaining carcass will be extremely thin at that point. It should go without saying that a tyre that has been worn through normal usage should be replaced as soon as possible.

Deflation can be complete or partial, and this is where tubed and tubeless tyres will behave differently. If punctured by a nail or thorn for example, a tubeless tyre will generally deflate more slowly as the carcass material will tend to self-seal around the penetrating object. However, if a tubed tyre is punctured similarly, then it will usually deflate quite quickly as the tube doesn't have the same ability to self-seal. It is best to leave the object in a tubeless tyre, letting the tyre technician remove it as and when the puncture is repaired. The converse applies with tubed tyres though, as it is possible that the penetrating object might also puncture the rim side of the tube as the pressure goes down. Likewise it's also possible that the object could rip the tube if left in place for too long, making any further repair impossible.

Tubed tyres are are vulnerable to 'nipping', or punctures caused by the tube being pinched between the tyre and the rim during an impact with a rock or hard ledge if being run at low pressure. Tubeless tyres won't suffer this fate as there's no tube to nip! Tubed tyres can be run at quite low pressures where necessary, as they can be secured to the wheel rim with 'rim-locks', which prevent the rim spinning inside the tyre. However, tubeless tyres cannot be run at such low pressures as a tubed tyre as they need a higher pressure to keep the tyre bead seated on the rim. If underinflated, there's a risk that the tyre might slip on the rim, break its bead, and possibly come off the wheel altogether.

↑ Daily maintenance is essential

📷 Adam Lewis

With both types of tyre a complete deflation is obvious and requires immediate inspection prior to repair, but a partial deflation is less obvious, and continuous use of an underinflated tyre will create a significant build-up of heat which could cause a catastrophic and instant failure of the tube, with potentially disastrous results.

Final drive to the rear wheel is generally by chain or shaft. Of the two, shaft drive requires little maintenance as it is a sealed, fixed-ratio unit that only requires work if a leak occurs because of seal failure, or as part of a regular schedule in which drive case oil levels are checked. A chain drive will require lubrication and adjustment throughout its life, but both tasks are relatively simple to perform. If

the bike is to be used in dry and sandy conditions then it should be left 'dry'. Most larger bikes' chains are of the 'X' or 'O' ring variety, with each link having its lubrication sealed within the pin and roller. If the bike is to be used in normal or wet conditions, then consider a chain lubricating system such as the Scottoiler, which automatically dispenses a small amount of oil on to the chain.

Other regular maintenance tasks within the reach of a reasonably competent mechanic include adjusting valve clearances on engines with screw/lock adjusters, and performing an oil and filter change. The air filter is also usually reasonably easy to access and should be at the least renewed before a tour and certainly cleaned if subjected to particularly dusty use. Desert dust can be extremely fine and will get into the smallest crevice on the motorcycle, which means that the air filter can become clogged after as little as 100km of dry piste riding. Dry paper elements are easily cleaned with an air-line and nozzle; oiled mesh or foam filters need washing in an appropriate solvent, drying, and re-oiling before replacing them. Air-filter 'socks' are available to slip over some filters (KTM Dual Air foam filters), which give a first line of defence and can easily be washed with your socks and pants after a long day in the dirt.

→ Keep the chain lubricated under normal or wet conditions

📷 Thorvaldur Orn Kristmundsson

Gear and equipment

Luggage

Soft luggage or hard luggage – the perennial question. If there is an iconic image of an overland motorcycle, then it will be a BMW GS equipped with Zega panniers and top-box. There is no doubt that hard luggage will be the natural choice of the majority of aspiring overlanders. For a long time hard luggage was only available in aluminium, but in recent years high-density polyethylene has emerged as a viable contender and has been used to good effect by Hepco & Becker with their 'Gobi' range of luggage. Both materials have their merits – light, stable, secure, and easily manufactured into rigid storage boxes. The 'Gobi' panniers have an innovative twin-walled design which not only increases rigidity, but also provides a very useful 3-litre water carrying capacity if the boxes are equipped with the necessary taps.

UK-based Metal Mule manufactures a range of extremely high quality aluminium boxes with cleverly thought out features such as concealed locks, cast silicone weatherproofing seals, and lids which hinge outwards from the bike providing a very useful work or eating surface. Fabric inner bags are available which allow the contents to be removed without taking the panniers off the bike. Hard luggage provides a high level of security and has a myriad of other uses, such as supporting the bike during wheel changes, or as impromptu seats or a table. It was even suggested by our Icelandic friends that the plastic Gobi boxes fitted to the F650GS offered a degree of buoyancy and support during deeper river crossings, but don't count on this to get you across! The inherent rigidity of hard luggage also affords a certain level of protection should the bike be dropped or crashed. Disadvantages are that systems can be heavy – they are undoubtedly bulky and can distort beyond use in the event of a heavy impact.

Soft luggage has a very different range of strengths

← **Custom luggage always looks the part!**
📷 BMW Motorrad

and weaknesses. Tank bags and tank panniers will usually be made from ballistic nylon or Cordura and offer a very convenient method of carrying items that need to be quickly accessible. Soft luggage has the benefit of flexibility (so odd-shaped items can be stowed quite easily) and lightness. It doesn't always need mounting hardware and is easily removable/transportable. The downsides are low security, as soft luggage cannot be effectively locked, and lack of rigidity, as it doesn't offer as much protection to the contents as a hard pannier might.

Baggage security will always be an issue for overlanders. Along with the appealing less developed nature of many countries they visit, there tends to be a culture where theft is more prevalent. When you stop in a village it's not uncommon to find yourself with a crowd of children surrounding you, and frequently there will be one or two who are determined to pry bits of luggage from your bike. A useful product to prevent this happening is 'eXomesh' which is an expanding net made from steel cable and secured by means of a draw-cord and padlock. Using any kind of security product, though, draws attention to your luggage and that it contains stuff worth protecting – which also means that it's worth stealing.

Helmet

As with any kind of motorcycle clothing, there is a huge range of crash helmets for the adventure rider to choose from. Full-face types are the predominant choice, largely by virtue of the extra protection they offer. Modern manufacturing methods and materials make today's helmets the best they have ever been, and even budget

models can offer outstanding levels of protection, but it is vital to consult a dealer experienced in fitting them correctly to ensure that you have the right size. For serious off-road use it is essential to select one with a peak – a must-have item if riding in bright or sunny conditions. Whatever your choice, it is wise to think of the future and make sure that the helmet can accommodate an intercom headset.

The Shoei Hornet-DS is a very good example of a dual sport helmet. It has an excellent rating and can be fitted precisely, thanks to a range of different-sized linings. These are removable and can be washed to ensure they stay fresh and pleasant – vital after a long day in the dirt. The main advantage of a helmet like the Hornet, however, is its flexibility. Essentially it is an evolution of an MX helmet, boasting an innovative visor system that allows the retention of the peak. The visor is removable to permit the use of goggles if preferred, as is the peak for road riding. The helmet has great internal space and an effective ventilation system to keep your head cool.

A regular MX helmet can also be a good choice, but its lack of a visor will mean using goggles for eye protection, which can be somewhat cumbersome and sometimes difficult to keep clean and mist-free.

Flip-front road helmets are also popular, giving the best of both worlds as you can ride with them open if it suits you, or they can be closed to give protection. They can, however, be quite noisy and are often much heavier than other types of helmet.

With any choice of helmet it is essential to consider its ease of use, whether you prefer double D-ring or buckle fasteners, the availability of visors, and the rating it achieved on the new SHARP (Safety Helmet Assessment and Rating Programme) test.

Clothing

Textile or leather? This is a question that is perennially difficult, if indeed possible, to answer. Clothing will always be a personal choice, but certain factors must be taken into consideration.

The primary function of motorcycle clothing is to protect its wearer – be it from temperature, rain, physical contact, etc. For many years the only choice was leather. Leather is durable, abrasion resistant, and quite breathable, but it can also be quite heavy and it is certainly difficult, if not impossible, to make totally waterproof. (Recently a treatment has been developed

that can be applied to leather to make it waterproof, but time has yet to prove its success.)

The many benefits of textile-based suits make them an ideal choice for a motorcycle overlander. Modern suits are extremely versatile and flexible, and usually have a modular construction which allows various elements of the system to be used according to needs. The outer suit will generally be constructed using ballistic nylon, and in some cases this can be reinforced with Kevlar to

give additional protection. Some suits have a composite construction using leather on high-wear areas such as shoulders and elbows of the jacket, the seat of the trousers, and the lower leg where it gives some protection from the exhaust system or abrasion against the frame. Zipped air vents will usually be found on the front and rear of the jacket, and on the arms, which can be opened or closed as suits the wearer. Armour, located at high impact points such as shoulders, elbows, and knees, will be found in the majority of suits. A back protector should be thought of as an essential and integral part of your jacket. If your jacket isn't fitted with one, they are readily available from motorcycle clothing retailers, either to fit the sewn-in pocket, or as a larger strapped-on item which gives a greater area of protection.

The second part of the system is the inner layer which provides the waterproofing. The inner suits are usually made from a breathable fabric to help prevent the build-up of perspiration. High-end suits will use GORE-TEX, but there are other materials, such as Sheltex, as used in some Hein Gericke suits. These systems are generally very good at providing a controlled environment within the suit and, when used in conjunction with a base layer of clothing made from 'wicking' or other 'technical' fabric, can keep things comfortable and dry. In colder weather the layering of thinner undergarments increases insulation without getting sweaty and uncomfortable. In a hotter climate the waterproof inner layer can be removed and, when worn with the vents open and a 'wicking' T-shirt, this gives a very welcome cooling effect.

Boots

There will always be a compromise to reach with boots and gloves. Although they offer vital protection to some of our most delicate and fragile extremities, they are items that so often go overlooked. It has to be said that some protection is better than none at all, and it's better to wear light gloves and walking boots, for example, than trainers and bare hands. However, there are quite a few options available that will offer good levels of protection without being too difficult to wear.

Boots are probably second only to a crash helmet in terms of protection importance. Your feet and lower legs are very close to the ground and are in the firing line of any stones or rocks thrown up by the front wheel, or of other hard obstacles like ruts or protruding roots. High leg boots are a must, and ideally should have plastic or nylon reinforcement panels to protect the vulnerable parts of the lower leg, namely the shin and ankle. Trials boots might look fairly rugged, but they will probably not be stiff enough to offer any protection to the ankle, and likewise a motocross boot's sole isn't intended to give grip so will have a very smooth and often flat surface with no instep or defined heel. Modern boots are constructed of an array of different materials, with leather being used less and less often.

The ideal overlanding boot will have panels on both front and rear of the leg protecting the shin and Achilles tendon area. They will also be articulated around the ankle joint, making them more comfortable to walk in, while at the same time giving great lateral support. They will have a steel shank to protect your instep while standing, and a rugged commando type sole with a well-

defined heel. Try several types of boot before committing yourself, and be sure to buy the ones that feel right. Don't be tempted to think that tight composite boots will ease with use, because they won't. A tightness that seems tolerable in the shop will surely become unbearable after three or four hours riding. The ankle joints might free off a little, but modern synthetic materials have very little give in them. Also, bear in mind that boots of this type are rarely waterproof, despite the makers' claims, and paradoxically the water that gets into the boots with ease takes an age to dry out. GORE-TEX boot liners are available which are surprisingly effective at keeping your feet dry and comfortable at the cost of being slightly more bulky than just socks alone, so consider this when making your decision.

← There is no substitute for a good pair of boots
📷 Waldo van der Waal

Gloves

There are many choices available when it comes to gloves, and sadly there's no one universal glove that will suit everybody. Clearly your choice of glove will be determined by the type of riding you intend to do – there's no point at all in using waterproof winter gloves on a desert tour, and likewise a late summer tour round the Alps will probably need more than just a goatskin summer glove. Your trip research should give you a good insight into what kind of glove will be appropriate. In any event, gloves should have knuckle and finger protection at the barest minimum. Padding on the palm of the hand will help prevent fatigue and bruising which can come from spending a long time on uneven roads or a corrugated piste. Motocross or enduro gloves will give high levels of protection but not at the cost of comfort and flexibility. They will generally be made from a combination of materials, leather for breathability and durability on the palms, elasticated textile panels for stretch and comfort, and rubber or plastic inserts for upper finger/knuckle protection. If you feel that you might need extra protection against the cold, a good investment is a pair of silk inner gloves, and they take up very little room in a jacket pocket.

← Lighter MotoX-style gloves give better feeling on the throttle
📷 Robert Wicks

Training schools

↑**BMW's training school in Germany where students are put through their paces**
📷 BMW Motorrad

There is no better place to improve your off-road riding skills than out on the trail, but for newcomers to adventure motorcycling, or for experienced riders wanting to learn more, the place to start is an off-road training school.

A quick search on-line, or a look in the classified section of a good off-road magazine, is where you will find many schools listed. Be sure to choose the one which can offer you what you're looking for, and ideally using the same or similar motorcycle to the one you own, assuming of course you cannot make use of your own bike.

Most off-road schools offer courses over a one- or two-day period at a bespoke training facility. If you haven't purchased all your riding equipment by the time you go training, many offer gear either as part of the course or for hire at reasonable prices. It's better, though not essential, to use your own equipment.

Most schools are run by private individuals, although in recent years some of the leading manufacturers have established their own facilities. One such school is the BMW Off Road Skills course in Wales where professional instructors teach participants the essentials of off-road riding, with the objectives of increased confidence and machine control, together with improved riding skills and, ultimately, the pure enjoyment of riding off-road. Run by seven-times Dakar Rally participant, Simon Pavey, the school caters for all levels from novice to expert. 'We aim to offer the full spectrum of training from novice to advanced, and at our unique facility in Wales riders can experience everything that awaits them on a real world adventure,' says Pavey. Key lessons include:

Being able to lift, balance, and manoeuvre a motorcycle in awkward situations – This is particularly relevant, given the variable terrain you are likely to cross.

Slow-speed manoeuvring and control – This is vital should you cross hazardous rocky terrain, and can even prove useful when negotiating your way through traffic in a bustling town.

Balance and control – An essential given the weight you are likely to be carrying, the terrain that will be covered, and places and spaces that you will have to negotiate with the bike.

Throttle and clutch control – This is as vital off-road as it is for anyone riding on the road. Proper throttle and clutch control makes a tremendous difference to how you handle the bike and how you cope in difficult situations.

Enhanced braking ability – Hazards on the roads are far more prevalent the further you move away from built-up areas, and your ability to brake hard and in a controlled manner off-road on a bike carrying considerable momentum is a fine art.

Ascending and descending hills – This can be intimidating at first, but being able to cope with these confidently is an essential skill which should be mastered particularly if you are headed into unknown terrain.

For more information about the Off Road Skills course, log on to **www.offroadskills.com**.

⬇**Instructor and student at the Off Road Skills course in Wales**
📷 Robert Wicks

⬆**A great way to learn how the bike reacts in a rut**
📷 BMW Motorrad

Training in the USA

At RawHyde Adventures, North America's premier training school for adventure riders, participants are offered an all-encompassing adventure experience, learning about riding their motorcycles in challenging conditions and spending several days immersed in the 'lifestyle' of adventure riding. Owner and founder, Jim Hyde, says: 'It's simple – in order to control the weight of a big adventure bike we must really interact with the machine to control it properly. This differs greatly from the techniques employed in normal street riding or traditional dirt riding.' At his school in California, Jim focuses on six key areas that make any off-road riding experience more enjoyable, and sets you on the right path to adventure.

Balance – It's a funny thing, many folks learned to ride a bicycle as a kid by running next to the bike and jumping on. This technique uses momentum to help with balancing the bike. Many riders think that momentum is still the key to riding. While you can get away with that on the street, you cannot do so in the dirt. Pure balance is the most important aspect of handling a big bike in the dirt. Most people never think about it because they have learned that momentum helps keep motorcycles upright. 'Unfortunately you can't go fast enough in the dirt to depend on momentum all the time. It is far more important to focus on balancing your bike with "technique" rather than momentum,' says Jim.

Slow down – 'You are not racing the Dakar Rally,' says Jim, and no matter what you think your bike is capable of, its weight is likely to toss you to the ground at the next ditch or rut. Big bikes don't stop too quickly, either, and all that weight will hurt if you can't stop before a rut or obstacle. 'You should ride your big off-road bike like you would drive a jeep – slow and in control,' he concludes.

Stand up on the pegs – Many riders are uncomfortable standing on the pegs in rough terrain. 'Give it a try. You would be surprised how natural it seems after only a short while,' says Jim. Here is the reason why we do it. Our feet are our body's natural way of balancing itself. Thus, it's easier to balance our bike by standing than sitting. Motorcycles bounce around when we ride off-road, and standing up lets us adjust our position on the bike much more quickly, thus helping to keep the machine balanced.

Stay loose and relaxed – The key to controlling an adventure bike is to use your body weight to make the machine do what you want, not the other way around. If you are tense and tight on the bike, you can't respond to the bike's movements. Your mass is added to the bike's weight, and when something happens you can't respond quickly. By being loose (and by standing on the pegs) you can let the bike move under you and use your body's influence when necessary.

➔ **Jim Hyde –
'It's all in the
technique',
he says**
 Rawhyde

Finesse with the clutch, throttle, and brakes – These three items are key, and you'll need to use them like never before. 'Can you ride around more slowly than first gear allows by slipping the clutch? Can you do it with very little throttle and not stall? Can you apply the brakes gently and come to a full stop, balanced, without putting a foot down? Then, can you use the controls to snap back into motion?' asks Jim. When going slow off-road, being in total control is crucial.

Know your limits – Everyone has limitations, based on size, height, strength, age, and experience. 'Be honest with yourself,' says Jim – adventure riding takes you to places where the roads are poor, hospitals are scarce, and resources are slim. 'Don't take chances, learn what you and your bike are capable of as a team and stick to what you are comfortable with,' he concludes. Wise words indeed.

For more information about RawHyde Adventures, log on to www.rawhyde-offroad.com.

Much of what you will learn at a training school appears on the pages of this book, but ultimately nothing beats being out on your bike learning new skills and developing your riding.

↑**Finish the course first before you take the instructor on!**
📷 BMW Motorrad

←**Doing exercises in a group helps to build your confidence**
📷 BMW Motorrad

We've all been through the process of learning to ride a bicycle, which has given us our skill to balance a two-wheeled vehicle. This balancing skill has, by and large, become innate in us, and we take our ability to do it for granted, particularly in the case of the road-going motorcycle. But, riding an off-road motorcycle requires a huge amount of physical and mental coordination, some we're aware of and some we're not. Instead of smooth and predictable tarmac, you will be faced with loose road surfaces, deep ruts, steep hills, and rocks and stones being thrown up at you, to mention just some of the challenges.

Jim Hyde says the six most common mistakes that street riders make when they hit the dirt for the first time are:

- Riding beyond their 'limits', don't know how to go slow, and ride too fast for the situation.
- Holding on too tight, are too tense on the motorcycle.
- Not realising the effect of sitting down versus standing up.
- Fixating on a particular target.
- Having a natural tendency to step away from what makes you nervous.
- Locking up the front wheel without knowing what to do.

These are all typical errors that, more often than not, can be dealt with through a new sense of balance. This might not come naturally at first, and it will require a conscious effort to think about and plan what you need to do. Acceleration, deceleration, and momentum are forces that you must constantly manage in order to maintain equilibrium and achieve progress from A to B off-road. When you get it right, the feeling of unity with the bike will be an absolute joy, but if you get it wrong the consequences could be more than just an embarrassing tip-over in a car park. With practice, though, your response to what the bike needs to keep it in balance will become more of an instinctive reaction. In this chapter we will explore some of the forces at work and how they affect the way we ride. ■

Balance and centre of gravity

The centre of gravity of an object is the point at which all forces act equally, or in other words the point around which the object is said to be in equilibrium or balance. An easy way to visualise this might be to imagine a cube with lines diagonally connecting opposite corners. The point at the centre of the cube at which these lines intersect is its centre of gravity. If the cube were to be suspended at that point it would hang in perfect balance, but if the suspension point were moved inside the cube, then balance would be lost and it would hang lopsided.

In his coaching manual on off-road riding, New Zealander Nick Reader comments: 'You have an imaginary point in your body around which your weight is evenly distributed, which tends to be around your stomach area. Your bike has a similar point around the middle of the engine. Controlling a motorcycle has a lot to do with where the two centres of gravity are in relation to each other, and the closer a rider can put their centre of gravity to that of the bike, the more stable, controlled, and balanced he or she will be.' A common mistake made, especially by off-road riders, is that riders sit too far back on their machines. This means their centre of gravity, and weight, is rear of the motorcycle's, which

in turn means the rider overloads the rear suspension, straining their forearms and back muscles.

In a perfect world the centre of gravity on a motorcycle would be equidistant between the axles giving an ideal 50/50 weight distribution on each wheel. In reality, however, it is rarely exact and in the case of a KTM 640 the distribution is 46% front and 54% rear. Add 30kg of luggage at the rear, and the figures change dramatically to 39% front and 61% rear, which can have a significant effect on the way the bike handles and reacts to different types of terrain. The height of a motorcycle's centre of gravity also has a noticeable effect on its handling. A simple way to illustrate this would be to visualise a broomstick with a sliding weight on it. With the weight towards one end of the stick it's easy to lift the other end of the stick – the stick acts as a lever and the effort required to lift the weight is low. Move the weight up the stick, however, and the leverage effect gets smaller and more effort is required to lift the weight.

A motorcycle with a low centre of gravity will feel quite stable and easy to manoeuvre at low speeds, and will be relatively easy to lift from its side. One with a higher centre of gravity will feel 'top-heavy' at lower

speeds, and the extra leverage needed to lift it from its side can make picking it up a bit of a challenge.

With the bike on the move, however, things become much more dynamic. The rider becomes an active part of the equilibrium equation and their input has a significant effect on how the bike reacts to changes in its position. Moving your body weight to one side of the bike will shift the centre of gravity in that direction, increasing the downward force applied to that side of the bike. Likewise, moving bodyweight forward increases the force on the front wheel, and moving back increases the downward force on the back wheel. We'll explore how you can make these forces work for you in greater detail elsewhere, but these subtle shifts in a rider's position can make all the difference to the stability and feedback the motorcycle gives, and to the way it behaves.

The science of motorcycle dynamics is hugely complex and involves topics such as centrifugal force, gyroscopic precession, and angular momentum, to name but three. Thankfully, in this section we can take a brief look at a couple of forces we're all familiar with, namely acceleration and deceleration, and see how they work around the centre of gravity when we're riding

off-road, leaving the really clever stuff to the physicists.

At the risk of stating the obvious, we feel acceleration as the force acting on us as we increase our forward speed, almost like being pulled backwards as the bike goes faster and faster. That force we feel pulling us backwards also generates a weight transfer to the rear of the bike, which can be seen as the fork-legs extend and the front of the bike lifts a little. Cracking the throttle open on a powerful bike can create sufficient rearward weight transfer to allow the front wheel to lift completely off the ground, and all of a sudden we've popped a wheelie! The process in reverse is deceleration, which we achieve by using the brakes. Applying the front brake will cause a weight transfer to the front wheel, the forks dip as the brake slows us down to stop. Apply the brakes too hard and the weight transfer can be so great that the rear wheel lifts off the ground in a 'stoppie' or, in the worst case, flips over the front wheel.

The bike's centre of gravity is very relevant in these situations. Where this is forward on the bike it will want to lift its rear under braking, and where it is rearward it will want to wheelie under acceleration. However, riders can compensate for this by moving their body mass – for example, pushing themselves backwards under braking

↑ Add luggage and that centre of gravity changes quite dramatically
📷 BMW Motorrad

Acceleration
Transfer body weight forward

shifts the overall centre of gravity backwards and helps stabilise the bike. Moving your body forward under acceleration shifts the overall centre of gravity forwards and increases the weight loading on the front wheel, keeping it planted on the ground.

With a rider aboard, the centre of gravity is no longer a static point. With the rider's weight applying a downward force on the foot pegs, the bike will tend to pivot around that point. By moving around on the bike, either standing or seated, the rider can shift the centre

of gravity to help the bike in certain circumstances.

An extreme example might be found when climbing a steep hill. With the driving force through the bike's rear wheel, the rear axle becomes a pivot point. If the rider were to move their weight backwards, the bike's centre of gravity would move to the rear, which reduces the downward force on the front wheel. As power is applied to climb the hill, this could lead to the front wheel lifting, making steering impossible at best, and at worst allowing the motorcycle to flip backwards. To counter this, the

Braking
Transfer body weight rearward

Cornering
Weight the outside peg

rider must lean forwards, moving the centre of gravity towards the front of the bike, which effectively increases the downward force on the front wheel and lessens its tendency to lift. With the wheel in firm contact with the ground, steering is maintained and upward progress can continue. It is a fine balance, though, as too little weight on the rear wheel will lead to a loss of traction as you climb the hill.

Turn the situation round, and look at a hill descent. On a downward slope and under front wheel braking,

the front axle is now the pivot. The rider's weight should be shifted rearwards to move the centre of gravity as far back as possible, reducing the tendency for the back wheel to lift by increasing the downward force acting on it. Increasing the downward force on the rear wheel also helps the descent by improving rear wheel traction and braking, which aids directional stability as well as taking some of the load off the front wheel, which in turn improves steering response at the same time as reducing the risk of a front wheel wash-out.

Sliding
Balance throttle and steering, with body weight well forward

Basic positions

There are two basic riding positions – seated or standing – although it can be difficult to know when properly to use either. This is one question that new adventure riders sooner or later will agonise over. Inevitably, the 'new' rider will venture off-road remaining seated while the going's good, occasionally standing on the foot pegs to have a stretch or a look round. In fairness, there's nothing wrong with that at all, but the reality is that there is so much more to be gained from knowing how to use those positions effectively.

Jim Hyde comments: 'Staying light on the bike is a concept that is difficult to understand until you have had some practice, but the fact is that motorcycles on dirt surfaces tend to dance around as you ride them. It can be unnerving, but the handlebars will shift from side to side as the wheels encounter bumps and ruts. This is a natural part of riding off-road, and if you are stressed or tense you will attempt to compensate for each shift and will actually cause yourself to fall much more often.'

By keeping a light steady 'guiding hand' on the bars, standing on the pegs, and gripping the tank with your knees, you can let the bike shift back and forth beneath you. 'You will quickly see that you do not need to compensate for each wiggle the bike makes – you will relax, and by doing so, the bike will stabilise even more,' says Jim. Holding tight on to the handlebars – whether seated or standing – prevents the bike from dancing, makes you much more unstable and rapidly wears you out.

Ultimately the key to comfortable and confident riding is having a flexible and neutral position or attitude on the bike, allowing you to conserve energy whilst still maintaining maximum control over the bike. This is usually the standing or 'attack' position, but staying seated on an easy stretch of track might be equally appropriate. Taking a look at these styles will reveal just how different they are, and will also illustrate precisely how they underpin the essential and advanced skills outlined in subsequent chapters.

Seated

Let's take a look at the seated position. In this situation, you are one with the bike, securely triangulated by your pelvis, shoulders and hands. It is the most natural position and certainly the most familiar if you are accustomed to riding a road bike. Using the seated position is best for easy going conditions. It allows you to rest and take in the scenery knowing that the road ahead is clear of obstacles. Remember that in the seated position your visibility is limited, so be certain of what lies ahead.

In terms of technique, initially position your body as centrally as possible. From here you will be able to feel the bike and you can then begin to adjust your position (and weight) either forwards or backwards to suit the situation. Keep your head in line with the centre of the handlebars and keep your elbows up for stability.

When seated, your weight is transferred to the bike via the seat and, likewise, the bike's movements are transferred via the seat to you. This is all well and good while you're riding a reasonable track – the suspension will do its job and isolate you from the imperfections of the road surface as long as they are not too severe. But once things get rough you will start to feel all the bumps and undulations coming through. As you are connected to the bike by your bum, those forces are transferred to you through the bike. All that jarring can become very uncomfortable and will inevitably divert your concentration from your riding. It's at this point that you need to think about standing up.

There are times when sitting on the bike can have a positive benefit – for example, riding through uncertain or concealed surfaces such as muddy ruts, or over an unpredictable surface such as snow. Riding with your feet down, or 'paddling', can at times give an increased sense of stability, helping to keep the bike upright, which in turn allows you to maintain forward momentum. When doing this it is important to be conscious of where you place your feet , making sure they do not get caught on anything.

Overall, it is important to remain flexible while seated – ride leaning slightly forward and with your elbows bent. This position gives you maximum control over the steering, whilst allowing you to move with the bike over difficult terrain.

➔ **Sit when the going is easy and regain some energy for when the going gets tougher**
📷 Robert Wicks

Standing

Riding in the standing position may not come naturally at first. To an off-road novice the saddle of a motorcycle represents a secure and stable place to be, but paradoxically the sense of stability and security can be increased by standing on the foot pegs. Flexibility and neutrality have been mentioned several times already, and riding on undulating terrain is where these attributes are most beneficial. When standing you have a much better view of the way ahead, giving you more time to react to road conditions. But there are much greater benefits to be had from standing.

In the previous section we mentioned the relationship between shoulders, pelvis, and hands. When standing, however, that triangulation is broken, allowing the rider to move around on the bike and, equally important, allowing the bike to move under the rider. This extra degree of freedom gives flexibility, and the ability to move the centre of gravity as required. Influencing the centre of gravity is paramount in being able to weight the wheels appropriately for the conditions, the terrain,

or the attitude of the bike. Simply standing on the pegs is the first step in actually being able to use that 'dynamic force' to your advantage.

Standing up affords the best level of control over the motorcycle and allows you to react on the motorcycle, rather than being acted upon as is often the case when seated. Shifting your weight around is much easier when standing, and very difficult when sitting.

In the basic standing position, the rider's body weight is applied equally to both pegs. Think of the foot pegs and your feet as a ball and socket joint whereby your hips are effectively disconnected from the bike, so when the bike moves the rider doesn't have to. Keep a gentle bend in your knees and bend slightly at the hips to connect with the handlebars. Bending the knees slightly gives the flexibility and shock absorption required to ensure maximum rider comfort and control.

Try to keep your hips in front of the foot pegs as this allows your leg muscles to stay with the bike as you accelerate. Similarly, by moving your hips just behind the pegs when decelerating means your upper body

← **By standing up the rider allows the bike to move around freely beneath him**
📷 Robert Wicks

■ Field of vision - **Seated**

↑**Standing dramatically enhances your field of vision**

📷 Thorvaldur Orn Kristmundsson

has less work to do under the force of braking.

Always keep your elbows up for strength and responsiveness. This not only allows more muscles to be engaged, but importantly allows proper throttle control as the bike moves about. Keep one or two fingers on the brake and clutch levers to maximise response time, and hold on to the handlebars with your other fingers.

In this basic position riders can maintain their body attitude while the bike moves around them. The importance of being able to do this will be shown in greater detail elsewhere, but this simple skill allows the rider to load either of the bike's wheels according to the conditions. For example, under acceleration we need two basic things: equilibrium and steering. By standing

and leaning forwards we move the centre of gravity towards the front which decreases the tendency of the front wheel to lift, but also increases the weight on the front wheel, thereby maintaining steering input. When leaning forwards, the arms are more relaxed giving much greater control over the steering.

Under braking the opposite is true. When the brakes are applied, a lot of weight is transferred to the front wheel. To maintain equilibrium you should look to push your hips backwards, moving the centre of gravity to the rear, thus reducing the weighting on the front wheel. As we'd generally only brake hard in a straight line it's fairly safe to keep your arms straight, bracing yourself against the handlebars. Doing this helps keep the bike stable by

■ Field of vision - **Standing**

increasing the weight on the back wheel and reducing the chance of the front wheel washing out.

The standing position is also the best to use for ascents and descents. Attacking a hill from the standing position lets the front of the bike rise while the rider stays in a more vertical position, pivoting on the pegs. This effectively moves the centre of gravity forwards, maintaining equilibrium by loading the front wheel, which keeps it in contact with the ground. Steering and rear wheel grip is maximised as you climb the hill. Turn this technique around and the same principles apply for descents. As the bike approaches the lip of the descent, push your hips back to move the centre of gravity backwards over the rear wheel.

When riding on some loose surfaces the bike will sometimes have a tendency to 'shimmy' or move about a little. This movement is caused by the loose surface moving under the bike's tyres, causing a small amount of lateral instability. This can be a little disconcerting, especially when seated, as the rider can feel every movement of the bike underneath him. However, standing on the footrests separates the rider's mass from the bike, allowing it to move freely over the road's imperfections while the rider remains in a stable and confident position above the bike. As you ride, maintain smooth throttle control, remember the position of your elbows, hips, and knees, and have a sense of where your wheels are at all times.

➜ **Stand up for a better view of what's in front of you!**
📷 Robert Wicks

Transitioning

The transition from the standing position to the seated position, and vice versa, should be executed as smoothly as possible. The key here is good forward observation. If you see a significant change in terrain in front of you it's likely that you will need to stand not only to tackle the route, but also to assess the road surface ahead, as well as your line. Aim to be standing for 10–15 seconds before the obstacle, as this will give you ample opportunity to identify any potential hazard and to adjust your speed and riding stance accordingly. It is unwise to transition when moving over rough or undulating terrain as this is when the bike needs to be at its most stable.

Remember that a transition either way results in a significant weight transfer and a rapid change in the centre of gravity, so aim to keep your body weight as balanced as possible on the bike as you do it.

To move from the seated position to the standing position, simply straighten your legs until you are standing on the bike with slightly bent legs. To move from the standing position to the seated position, sit and slide forward in the same motion until you are sitting as far forward or as far back as required by the situation. Always strive to maintain even pressure on the pegs to prevent any unnecessary imbalance.

1

Approach the hazard in a stable seated position

2

Aim to transition smoothly...

3

📷 Robert Wicks

...to a flexible standing attack position

Riding pillion

Off-road riding with a pillion is a fantastic way of sharing the excitement of overlanding with someone, although riding with the added complexities of a passenger takes a little thought and there needs to be a unique level of understanding between rider and passenger for the experience to be a happy one.

Riding with a passenger aboard requires some consideration from both parties. The rider must allow for the passenger's weight affecting the performance of the motorcycle, particularly with respect to braking. They should try to make the ride as smooth as possible, with braking and acceleration not so harsh as to cause the pillion to have to work too hard or clash helmets. The passenger must try to remain in a stable position on the motorcycle, and should only twist from the waist, as using their hips or pelvis will upset the balance of the bike, making life difficult for the rider. The passenger should be able to brace themselves either on the motorcycle, or preferably by holding each side of the rider's waist. If the passenger holds the rider, they should do so with a fairly light but firm grip, but never with a 'bear-hug', as this simply locks rider and passenger together preventing either from being able to move freely, making for a very stiff and jolting ride. A lighter grip allows the passenger to feel how the rider is moving and reacting to road conditions, and use those cues to move in harmony with them. If the terrain is bumpy, then the pillion can stand slightly, just enough to lift themselves off the seat, which will allow the motorcycle to move without jarring or jolting their spine.

Obviously, there will be more challenging sections which would be more difficult if not impossible to ride with a pillion. In these cases the safety and well-being of both rider and passenger is paramount, so it would be prudent to ask the pillion to dismount and rejoin after the obstacle. In less demanding circumstances, riding with a pillion is much easier and it's an experience which is a pleasure to share.

BMW Motorrad

As typical adventure riding generally takes place over varying types of terrain, it is essential to understand beforehand as much as you can about all the different surfaces you are likely to encounter, so that you will know what to expect and can hone the skills you need to tackle them with confidence.

Remember, though, that irrespective of the terrain type, the key to riding off-road is keeping your head up. Look forward down the track, focusing at least 15-20 yards in front of you. You need to be constantly making assessments in advance so that you can firmly point your bike where you want it to go. It is impossible to pick the best line ahead by looking down at your front wheel.

Each surface type brings with it a different set of challenges and, by following the principles set out earlier in the book, you must keep in total control and make the most of any opportunity to minimise fatigue. For, even though you may be exercising the best technique, certain types of terrain, by their very nature, will be quite draining. You need to be aware of this at all times.

Whether you are spending time on long open gravel roads, crossing rivers, or attempting a tough mountain trail, each surface type requires specific skills and this chapter looks at them in some detail and explains what you can expect when out on the trail. ■

↓Always ride within your limits on gravel
📷 Touratech

It is quite likely that much of your time will be spent on gravel roads, and when joining them you should always take the head-on approach. If you move on to a gravel road from a turn there's a danger of your front wheel slipping away, particularly if you are riding at speed, as you make the transition to the looser surface.

Every attempt should be made to use that part of the track that has fewer loose stones and sharp edges. Always apply the basic rule – look up and look ahead – so that you spot any bad patches before you actually come to them, and can choose a path that offers the best traction. Looking anywhere but where you want to go is a mistake. Keep a steady throttle, and stand up whenever necessary. If you find car tracks, it's probably worth riding on them as the gravel is likely to be more compacted there.

Focus on your riding stance – it should be stable but not rigid, balanced but not unyielding. Try to feel the effect of the loose surface on the way the bike handles. If you've

not ridden on gravel before, tuck your knees around the tank for added stability and gradually lower your feet to skim just across the top of the surface. This technique should give you some reassurance, but be careful not to drag your feet over uneven surfaces as you could seriously injure yourself should your boot catch on a root or rock. As you gain confidence, try riding in the standing-up position. This transfers your weight on to the pegs, and ultimately will assist your balance.

Keep a light but firm grasp on the handlebars – your arms should be relatively loose and flexible. Though at first rather disconcerting, the front wheel must have some freedom to move – not too much, but some – and if

Gravel

you don't concede a little, the wheel will take it anyway, especially if the surface is loose.

Experienced riders might prefer to travel fast on gravel, but for novice and intermediate riders a moderate level of speed is more appropriate. Find a speed you are comfortable with and try to maintain as steady a pace as the terrain allows.

If you do hit an uneven patch of gravel, this is your cue to slow down. That way you have room to gently accelerate through the bad section without starting to go too fast. If you find the bike moves around a bit, accelerate a little more and it will steady up. If the road surface becomes more technical, push down harder on the foot

pegs, allowing the bike to move around freely beneath you as it crosses over the uneven surface. Grip the bike lightly with your knees, with your legs bent and your upper body moving freely.

Nervous braking on gravel can easily lead to a crash, so use the front brake with caution. In fact, don't brake at all unless you must; and if you must, then just a light application should be sufficient. If not, you're probably riding too fast. Sharp braking or snapping the throttle shut will only cause the wheels to lose even more traction.

Finally, make sure you ride within your limits and try to stay relaxed – this will help you to manoeuvre the bike and conserve your energy.

© Yamaha

Sand

Riding on sand can often be very disconcerting, largely because of a lack of front-end grip. The front of the bike feels 'loose' and almost seems to have a mind of its own. Sand riding can also be extremely tiring if the incorrect technique is applied. It can sap your energy very quickly with a resultant loss in your level of control.

The most important thing to remember is that momentum is your best friend. By keeping the bike moving forward you will make efficient progress, conserve energy, and maintain the degree of control you need.

A natural tendency when moving on to sand from a harder surface is to immediately change from the standing to the seated position where the bike can feel more 'planted' and the whole experience can seem less disconcerting. Another almost natural reaction can be to ease off on the throttle when it feels like the front wheel is going to wash out – this will make it worse. Keeping the throttle open and pushing your hips back lifts the front wheel out of the soft sand, propelling you forward and giving you control over the line you are trying to follow. This is where you will find the bike to be tremendously responsive to steering input from pressure on the foot pegs, and how much control can be gained from leg and hip movements.

If you know you are about to ride through miles of deep desert or beach sand, you will require a bit of preparation. First you will need to reduce your tyre pressures significantly, at the same time being conscious that this may cause the rear tyre to slip on the wheel rim unless you have a rim lock fitted. Slow down, and as you move on to loose sand gently tap into the power. Ride steadily with your elbows away from your body and your hips pushed well back, and allow the bike to move around beneath you. If necessary, speed up a little if the bike moves around too much. Should the sand become really deep, try your best not to stop. It is very important to keep moving, even if you have to paddle with your feet or jump off the bike and run beside it for a short stretch. Digging bikes out of the sand is an energy-sapping exercise, and the heavier your bike the greater the chance of getting stuck.

In very soft sand it is easy to dig a trench with the rear wheel and get stuck. If this happens, don't keep spinning the rear wheel. Use a rocking motion, backwards and forwards and, when ready, accelerate and drive out the other side of the trench. If this doesn't work, don't abuse your clutch by trying to power the bike out. Instead turn the engine off and lie the bike down on its side. Fill the holes left by the wheels with sand and try to compact the sand with your feet. Pick up the bike, start it, and get it moving before you jump aboard.

On a final note, remember that sand-riding really punishes your bike. Sand gets into every little nook and cranny. It will wear out moving parts a lot quicker than normal. Make sure you wash your bike thoroughly as soon as possible after a sand ride, and always clean the air filter. Pay specific attention to components such as the chain and sprocket (not an issue on a shaft-driven bike) but be sure the parts are clean before using a lubricating spray – a thick lube and dirty chain will leave sand clinging to it.

← **Always try to keep moving in the sand – momentum is your best friend**
📷 Waldo van der Waal

← **Get used to coming off in the soft stuff**
📷 BMW Motorrad

↑↑Allow the bike to move around beneath you and move your hips slightly back
📷 BMW Motorrad

↑It's very important to keep moving, even if this means getting off and running with the bike
📷 BMW Motorrad

Once you've got the hang of riding through sand, the next major challenge involving sand, and lots of it, is tackling the dunes. Like it or hate it, there will be a day when you have to ride over a dune rather than go round it. Riding dunes can be one of the most exhilarating experiences of a desert tour but, as with much off-road riding, success depends on technique as it is an extremely unstable environment. There are many different types of sand, some so fine it will literally swallow your bike and send you flying over the handlebars if you aren't careful.

Riding in the dunes is not only physically challenging (you will soon find out just how tiring it can be when you start having to pick your bike up every few minutes), but it also requires a great deal of concentration when it comes to navigation. By the very nature of dunes, it is easy to become disoriented. Add to this the likely heat and lack of water, and the environment you face is significantly challenging. Writing in *Chasing Dakar*, Scot Harden comments: 'Efficiency is the key to riding in sand dunes. Most riders complain that having to pick up a rally bike in the sand is one of the most physically exhausting exercises they encounter during the Dakar Rally. Often the heart rate reaches a maximum, picking up the bike. Save energy and remember to drink regularly from your hydration system.'

In terms of general technique, momentum is all important, and you should always be ready to accelerate when you feel the sand getting softer and the bike starting to sink in. Reduced tyre pressures can be helpful – softer pressures allow the tyre to deform and spread more in the

Dunes

same way as a camel's toes do (and camels seem pretty adept at desert crossings). With a greater footprint the tyre gets maximum traction on the soft sand. The softer the sand surface the less tyre pressure required.

Like any hill climb, getting up a dune requires speed, commitment, and courage – and the upside is that falling off in soft sand doesn't always hurt too much! You'll probably make a couple of approaches to get the feel of the bike as it starts going up the slope. Push your weight back enough to aid traction and help prevent the front wheel digging in, but not so far that you let the front come right up. Gripping the tank with your legs can help to brace your body position as and when the front digs into the sand.

Remember that sand saps the power from the engine and is very hard on your clutch, so be prepared to use

plenty of revs and plenty of throttle to keep the engine in its power band. Attack the dune at an angle (many are simply too soft to take head on) and maintain enough momentum to get to the top, always conscious of what awaits you on the other side, which could be anything from a steep drop to another rider, or yet another climb. Coming at the dune from an angle also gives you a better perspective as to what lies over the other side and buys you a little time to decide about whether to go over the top, continue along the crest of the dune, or return to the bottom.

On the down slope you will need to keep under power to prevent the wheels digging in. Move your weight backwards, stand up, and maintain momentum by using engine braking rather than the actual brakes as you descend.

↑ **Dune riding takes its toll on man and machine**
📷 BMW Motorrad

↓ Sometimes the cautious approach is best – moderate your crossing with the clutch
📷 Thorvaldur Orn Kristmundsson

Crossing rocks can be a tricky exercise and caution is called for, particularly if the rocks are large and unstable. Arguably the biggest issue to overcome is the actual fear of crossing rough and uneven ground. More often than not inexperienced riders, when confronted with it, will tend to slow down to a crawl and then attempt to 'paddle' across the rocks with both feet touching the ground. Small rocky outcrops can usually be crossed by adopting the standing position (for maximum visibility), choosing a good line, and applying a healthy dose of commitment. It's equally important that your elbows and knees are responsive to the uneven surface at all times in order to maintain control of the bike.

It's vital to choose the most direct route, as the combined actions of negotiating tough terrain and trying to turn the bike at the same time will tire you out more quickly and make a challenging crossing even more difficult. Keeping the front wheel pointed straight ahead will generally help with stability. Remember that sometimes avoiding the larger rocks or obstacles is not necessarily to your advantage. Occasionally, larger rocks, though potentially more challenging to negotiate, may offer more stability, so it is important to factor this into the choice of line – sometimes, rather than going around them, riding directly over rocks and debris will actually be the easier and more stable route.

Your suspension is there to absorb the shocks, so let it do its job. This, together with a neutral body position, will allow you to stay in control as the bike moves across obstacles of varying sizes. Commit as you set off, and move your concentration on to the next challenge. If you focus on the line and the bike's momentum and speed, the suspension will do the rest.

The clutch should be used to minimise wheel spin and maintain traction over the rocks. Moderating speed is extremely important in these conditions. The more momentum you maintain, the smoother the ride is going to be. By maintaining an even speed you enhance your ability to balance effectively, and thereby increase your control over the motorcycle.

When the ground is loose, the front brake needs to be used with caution. If you feel the front wheel dig into the ground, you are squeezing the lever too hard and you'll know it is time to ease off on the brake. Always be conscious of this over rough terrain as you can easily lose the front of the machine and go down in a heap.

If you find that the rocks are too challenging to ride across, it's time to get off the bike, assess the best way across and then proceed to walk the bike over. Having at least one other person with you is really useful in this instance. The bike will feel heavy and cumbersome, and it will be a much easier crossing with someone else to share the load. Once you have established the best line, slowly start moving forward with the engine running. Use all the controls – brake, throttle, and specifically the clutch, to moderate your progress. Look carefully where you place your feet, as losing your balance could result in the bike falling on top of you.

⬆ **Stay focused and keep the front wheel pointing forward**
📷 F J Maré

⬅ **Large rocks offer increased stability but watch out for slippery patches**
📷 Touratech

SIMON SAYS...

- Try to pick a good line which offers the most grip
- Enter the muddy ground in the standing attack position
- Keep up plenty of revs and try to maintain speed and momentum
- Your bike may also overheat during a period of slow riding and higher than normal revs, so check the radiator to ensure that it is not caked with mud
- Trying to ride around a muddy patch does not always work, and some people are known to have got stuck even worse when they tried to ride around a mud puddle when the ground next to the puddle couldn't support the weight of the bike
- If in doubt, walk it first. If you can't stand on it, you probably can't ride it
- If you do get stuck, jump off quickly and push with the bike in first gear

Mud

5

Riding in unpredictable conditions such as mud generally means less traction to count on, hence less control. Unlike more stable surfaces, riding on mud means you will need to plan further ahead for any change in speed or direction, and to then make this change at the appropriate time. Be aware that mud conceals what's underneath, so be prepared for unexpected ruts and boulders.

Generally speaking, there are no secrets or easy answers for a rider wanting to move a heavily-laden adventure bike through mud. Technique can vary from standing up, through to a lot of paddling with your feet as you proceed. Be prepared to take your time – moving through thick mud an be a slow process.

If the mud is not too deep and you can still stand up, use the neutral position. If you feel you are losing traction, then shift your weight to the back of the bike to help the rear wheel grip and drive. If you are losing steering control, then try to move forward to put more weight on the front wheel, helping it to grip and steer. If you do feel the bike moving about, remember that you can move and adjust your bodyweight to compensate. The principle of keeping the tyres perpendicular to the surface is most important here, as even a slight angle can send you sprawling. In muddy ruts, always try to align your body and the bike so that you are not fighting the edge of the rut, but try to keep the front well weighted to maintain grip and steering control.

A gung-ho approach of blasting at speed through a long patch of mud seldom works for bigger bikes. Instead, commit, look up and ahead, and aggressively keep the bike moving at a brisk walking speed. Steering control in loose conditions resides in the legs and hips, and you will find the bike is tremendously responsive to peg inputs.

Carrying a degree of safe speed will always help in these conditions, and linked to this is the need, where possible, to use open, flowing lines which will help to maintain your speed.

← **A mile or two like this – with very little grip – can be very tiring**
📷 Joe Pichler

↓ **Keep the bike moving and be aware of what lies beneath**
📷 Touratech

Rivers

6

It's possible that you may not need to cross a single river on your trip, but in a country like Iceland it's a regular occurrence. Never treat river crossings lightly. They can be treacherous, and the risks are exacerbated when trying to cross with a heavily-laden adventure bike. Don't underestimate the power of flowing water.

First and foremost, one should never plunge into a river without investigating the crossing. If possible, view the river from above to try to identify the shallowest and smoothest area of the riverbed, avoiding submerged boulders and other obstacles. It is not advisable to attempt a crossing if large pieces of debris, such as logs and branches, are being carried downstream. Two other important things to consider are the depth of the river and the speed at which it is flowing.

If you are happy with the conditions, pick a point on the opposite bank and walk towards it, looking and feeling for obstacles as you go. Try to keep the crossing as short as possible wherever you can. If it looks good, return for your bike and ride it through the route you have just walked. If the river is flowing fairly fast, use the current to your advantage by riding diagonally downstream, letting it help push you forward rather than fighting upstream against the flow.

Crossing a river is about balance and smoothness. Use the momentum of the bike to easily and smoothly move

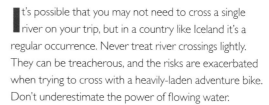

⬇ **Keep the bike upright and moving forward**
📷 Thorvaldur Orn Kristmundsson

📷 Thorvaldur Orn Kristmundsson

forward. If the bike bucks, moderate your progress with the clutch and throttle to keep the bike upright and moving – momentum through the water is vital.

If the riverbed is uneven and the river crossing challenging, remove your luggage and other kit first. Carry this over by hand to the far side of the river and then return to bring the bike across. A slow moving motorcycle that is bucking around needs to be as light as possible.

With or without luggage, the best body position is standing up, maintaining maximum visibility of the river-bed for any obstacles. Your body should be relaxed, arms easy, body balanced, legs bent. Gently power towards the chosen spot on the opposite side of the bank, making a small bow wave with the front wheel. If the bow wave starts to wet your upper body then you are going too fast and you will fall off should the bike hit an awkward spot.

When a river is flowing strongly, don't stand up and try to ride across – instead stay seated and, using your legs, paddle the bike across to the other side – getting your boots wet is a small price to pay for a safe crossing.

If for any reason you are uncertain or uncomfortable with the conditions, get another rider to walk through with you. Careful control of the throttle and clutch will be needed, with your helper supporting the bike in one of three positions – on the opposite side to counter-balance you, pushing from behind, or pulling from the front. Communication is essential throughout the crossing so both parties know what is happening during the crossing.

Generally, a riverbed offers a hard surface (otherwise the river would become a swamp) so don't worry about thick mud at the bottom. You may, however, find some mud right next to the banks of a river, so gently power through these areas. Riverbeds are also generally made up of stones with smooth edges, so you can deflate your tyres by 30–50% for more traction during a wide and difficult crossing.

On a final note, be conscious of your line if you are following a 4x4 or other vehicle across a river. A four-wheel vehicle will disturb the surface far more than your motorcycle ever will. Depending on the type of riverbed, what often happens is that an 'ideal line' is created just to the outside of where the 4x4 has crossed as stones are pushed sideways and out by the vehicle.

> **The single biggest risk attached to water crossing is the danger of completely submerging the bike, effectively 'drowning' it. For tips see:**
> ### Getting out of trouble on page 112

How to cross a river

1

Inspect the river crossing before making an attempt

2

If you're uncertain, it's safer to walk the bike over

Remove your panniers to lighten the load

Paddle through in the seated position if you're not comfortable standing up

↑ A case of tunnel vision?

📷 Globebusters

→ Don't lower your level of concentration when you come off the dirt

📷 KTM

Riding on sealed roads, with the smooth sensation of the asphalt passing beneath you without a rut in sight, can often bring some welcome relief after days or weeks off the beaten track. But, just because you have left the trail, it doesn't mean for a minute that you can drop your guard. Riding on the road, particularly in Third World countries, can be amongst the most hazardous riding you will encounter. With everything from erratic drivers, pedestrians, animals, fuel spills, and potholes to contend with, riding on such roads needs focus and awareness at all times.

Generally speaking, you can ride in the seated position, but don't hesitate to stand up if you need to improve your vision. Keep in mind that your safety is within your control and constantly look out for the unexpected so that you can take evasive action well in advance of any obstacles. It is vitally important at all times to monitor your likely stopping distance – always ride so that you maintain a clear view of your path ahead throughout your likely stopping distance. This, of course, is a general rule that applies wherever you are riding, and you should try to adopt a riding style that allows the maximum safety margin in any situation.

Whether in a town or out in the country, an asphalt road surface can present a number of hazards, as Mark Hodson, a motorcycle instructor and founder member of London Advanced Motorcyclists, points out:

Water

When it's raining, you naturally accept that the surface is wet and offers less grip, especially after a long dry spell, so you ride accordingly, leaving an increased separation for braking, and tackling bends and junctions more slowly. But during dry weather you may still encounter water on the road surface. Keeping an eye on the clouds will give early warning of wet roads ahead caused by an isolated cloudburst, and remember that long after rain has stopped falling you may still come across water dripping on to the road under bridges, gantries, trees, underpasses, and in tunnels. Also, vehicles will carry water into tunnels for a hundred yards or more. Incidentally, wet patches on dry roads are often more visible in the dark because they reflect light sources.

↑ **There is always something to think about around the next bend**
📷 Globebusters

→ **It's close to the edge but there is probably better grip in that area**
📷 Nick Plumb

SIMON SAYS...

- Always be conscious of setting off on cold tyres
- Take a quick glimpse over your shoulder before making a move in traffic
- Always approach intersections cautiously and with room to take avoiding action or to make a successful emergency stop
- Always be conscious of passengers alighting from a bus or the back of a truck and stepping into the road
- Be cautious of accelerating quickly from an intersection without checking for vehicles that might jump the red light and cross your intended path
- If there's a biker following you and you spot danger on the road surface, point to it, to alert them

↑ **Time to stop and make a snowman**
📷 Dennis Kavish

Frost

This shouldn't present you with too many surprises, as it is reasonably visible. It's usually encountered in the morning, melts slowly during the warmer daylight hours, and may reappear as darkness falls. Because it only occurs in very cold weather when you'll be aware that your tyres are also very cold and don't offer their maximum grip, you shouldn't come upon an area of frost riding fast and leaning far over on a bend. Remember too that the sun's movement means an area now enjoying sunshine may have been in the shade until 30 minutes ago. If you're uncertain about the amount of grip available, an exploratory dab with your boot on the road surface can tell you a lot. This is a useful technique worth practising, but remember it's always done with your foot behind, or to the outside of the footrest, never in front of it.

Ice

This presents the ultimate surface hazard, and grip is virtually non-existent. It can be expected to form initially on stretches of the carriageway that are exposed to the cold from underneath as well, such as flyovers and bridges. Dips in the road may hold frozen puddles, and openings in walls and hedgerows will permit cold wind to blow across and chill the road surface. Listen to the weather forecasts; they may predict a sudden cold spell following rain. A bird bath or a jar of water placed in the garden will confirm below zero overnight temperatures before you get on the bike in the morning. Watching vehicles ahead for unusual movements, such as snaking, or sliding down the camber, can provide early warning of ice but, ultimately, if you have reason to believe that ice is probable, there's no justification for riding.

Snow

Falling snow is horrible stuff to ride through. Apart from the disturbing visual effect, it can obscure lamps and indicators, screens, and visors within a hundred yards or so. Using your glove to wipe them will lead to a frozen hand within a few miles, and nothing mists up so readily as the inside of a visor that has snow on the outside. The effects of snow settling on the road surface can be rapid and dramatic. Road signs, cat's-eyes, road markings of all sorts, and even the kerbs can become obscured in minutes. This can lead drivers to believe they have right of way across your path when they don't, and you could make the same mistake. And don't forget that some pedestrians suddenly prefer walking in the road to walking on the pavement when there's snow on the ground. There are different types of snow. The sort that's good for snowballs because it sticks together so well, will fill in the tyre tread pattern and quickly build up under the mudguard. This leads to a lessening of grip on the road surface and a growing braking effect from the compacting snow between the tyre and guard. The result will be that the wheel stops turning. If snow is settling rather than melting, all of the considerations relating to ice apply.

← **Get the kettle on, will you!**
📷 Alex Murariu

↑ **Time to stop and make a snowman**
📷 Dennis Kavish

Mud

Mud varies in colour and character depending on soil type. Our interest lies in being able to predict where it will be found on the carriageway. In the countryside you expect to come across mud on the road fairly often. It's likely near farms, fords, field gates, forestry tracks, and on lanes with high banks on either side, particularly during and after rain. But in urban areas mud on the road is uncommon enough to catch you out unless you can predict its presence. Road works will often lead to mud on the surface, and warning signs should be erected by the contractors, though they may be blown over if it's windy.

Wet leaves

Wet leaves offer almost no grip, and this condition persists long after it's stopped raining. This is because the top layers prevent evaporation, and hence drying, from the lower layers. Although it might seem obvious that their presence could be predicted by the time of year and the proximity of trees, remember that, when dry, leaves can be blown some distance.

Grit

Grit, gravel, litter thrown from vehicles, cigarette ends and wind-blown debris tend to migrate to the kerbside, and the middle of the road around traffic islands, bollards, and the central reservation. These are the areas not driven over by other vehicles but only by cyclists and ourselves when filtering through heavy traffic to gain advantage. Obviously, this debris offers a poor braking surface. Also it

offers poor grip to the sole of your boot and this creates a problem when you filter right to the front, along the outside of a line of traffic, to be first away at the lights. On a machine with a high centre of gravity (or a full fuel tank) there's a strong possibility of toppling over as your supporting foot slides away from you. This is one of the rare instances where it's acceptable to use your left foot for support, with the bike in gear and the front or rear brake held on.

Fuel spills

These are a frequent cause of motorcycle accidents. With petrol we're at least comparatively fortunate that the fairly rapid evaporation of the fuel limits the risk, but diesel fuel doesn't evaporate readily, so it presents a more lasting danger. Spillages are mainly due to ill-fitting or missing filler caps. When the vehicle negotiates a bend, a roundabout or a junction, fuel surges towards the outside of the vehicle and may escape from the filler neck. You have to expect fuel spills near filling stations, bus and coach depots, and the yards of haulage contractors and other operators of fleet vehicles who may have on-site refuelling facilities. Leaks from the fuel line, filter housing, pump or injectors can deposit the substance anywhere on the carriageway, and concentrations will occur where the vehicle has been slow moving or stationary. An obvious point is that if you come across a fuel spill on, say, a left-hand bend, you can expect more on successive left-hand bends.

Animal droppings

These can pose a foreseeable hazard in the countryside where not only farm animals but wildlife too is ever present. Cattle markets and abattoirs are also obvious sources of the problem.

Debris

Encountering debris on the carriageway is something many riders don't seem to accept as a possibility, let alone a probability. Get used to it – in Third World countries on an adventure ride, it's a regular occurrence. Old traffic cones, the carcasses of lorry tyres, dead animals, and complete or partly smashed pallets are commonplace, as are parts of exhaust systems and wheel rims. Any item that can be carried on an open-backed lorry or pick-up truck (both of which are common in remote areas for moving people and goods) can fall off the back, particularly where the road surface is poor, or at a hump-

↑ **Give way to buses! Be mindful of driving standards in other countries**
📷 Danny Burroughs

← **Keep an eye out for local wildlife**
📷 KTM

backed bridge. At places where the vehicle follows a curving path, items may fall sideways, so be cautious when overtaking. It may be asking a lot, but try to have some idea of the surface presented to people coming the other way too. They may swerve to avoid something, or skid towards you. And if you'll be coming back that way soon it's nice to have advance warning of possible trouble spots.

↑No falling rocks or goats to contend with here – Iceland at its best

📷 Thorvaldur Orn Kristmundssonr

Few countries in the world offer the unique and varied terrain that Iceland does. The appropriately named Biking Viking Motorcycle Tours company offers guided tours of the country on BMW motorcycles. The company was founded in 1998 by Njall Gunnlaugsson, a long-time motorcycle enthusiast. 'We often refer to Iceland as the motorcycle playground of the gods as the country has more gravel roads than most other countries,' says Njall. The country also offers river crossings, lagoons, sand, highland routes, glaciers, waterfalls, volcanoes, geysers, and even twisty asphalt roads.

Biking Viking tours are generally undertaken on BMW's capable F650 machines, the characteristics of which make it the ideal choice for adventure riding in Iceland. The company offers a range of tours to meet the needs of riders with different skills levels and interests. One of their most popular expeditions around Iceland takes in all the country has to offer:

Biking Vikings

Day 1

From Reykjavik we head to the south coast to the spectacular Seljaland and Skogarfoss waterfalls. The route passes along two glaciers and then to accommodation located beneath, Vatnajokull, the largest glacier in Europe.

Day 2

After breakfast to the Jokulsarlon (glacier lagoon) for a boat tour and lunch. The rest of the day is made up of a ride along Vatnajokull to the eastern fjord of Iceland with its magnificent mountains and valleys.

Day 3

The route then heads north-east on gravel roads through one of Iceland's biggest forests, passing through spectacular scenery on the way to Vopnafjordur and then to Bakkafjord-East.

Day 4

The route leads to Asbyrgi, one of nature's wonders. It is a 3½km long canyon with 100m high cliff walls. It was created by two catastrophic flood waves from the Vatnajokull icecap. Then, on to the most powerful waterfall in Europe, Dettifoss, and overnight at Lake Myvatn.

Day 5

After a visit to the capital town of the north, Akureyri, the route heads down across an old highland road.

Day 6

Some great off-road riding leads west to the Snaefellsnes glacier, and shark meat is on the menu for lunch.

Day 7

Return to Reykjavik, routing along the volcanic mountains of the Snaefellsnes peninsula.

biking viking
MOTORCYCLE TOURS
ICELAND

For more information, visit **www.bikingviking.is**

Dakar veteran Scot Harden is quoted as saying 'the most important performance modification to a motorcycle is to improve the skills of its rider.' Many making the change from a sports bike to an adventure bike are likely to find it a bigger step than initially anticipated. Instead of a nimble, lightweight machine that's easy to get on and off, adventure bikes are heavier, can be more cumbersome, and need to be ridden in a particular way to get the best out of them. Add to this the unpredictable terrain and conditions one is likely to encounter, and there is every reason to be suitably skilled.

On the trail, the situations you are likely to face will be far more complex and challenging than normal road riding. Accordingly, you will need your responses to these situations to happen more 'automatically', with many becoming almost second nature. Of course, your reaction time will be longer if you're tired, cold, unfit, or simply not concentrating.

Off-road riding does not present us with smooth and predictable tarmac, it throws rocks and stones at us, it gives us loose road surfaces, deep ruts and steep hills, to mention but a few. Each of these obstacles can be overcome with a degree of skill and, more important, the right technique, and we shall explore some of the possibilities.

The skills outlined here are designed with two key things in mind – to give you maximum control of the bike and to minimise fatigue – the two most important attributes of adventure riding other than having fun. Obviously, each type of surface requires a certain technique, but in general, the following basic tips are always worth bearing in mind.

If you can apply these tips to your riding and develop the actual skills to the point that they become second nature, then much of your mental and physical energy can be spent further ahead as new challenges present themselves on the trail. This chapter explains the various skills you need – from simply getting on to and off a heavily-laden adventure bike, to more complex skills such as confidently climbing steep hills. ■

ESSENTIAL RIDING TIPS

Constantly monitor the road surface for changing conditions and obstacles

Look up and look ahead, not down – you need to look beyond your front tyre

Think several steps ahead, always looking past and beyond obstacles and not fixating on any one thing

Momentum is often your best friend and it's vital to keep up a degree of speed even if the surface deteriorates

Do not constantly fight the bike's movement beneath you – instead allow the motorcycle to move around to find the best traction.

Lean forward – arms relaxed and bent, legs and inner thighs lightly gripping the motorcycle, soles of the feet firmly on the foot pegs

Always choose a good line and speed around a corner with loose material.

Stand up on the pegs for technical sections and sit when the going is easier (many people do it the other way round)

Use the stopping power (engine braking) of the gearbox

Always try to keep the bike perpendicular to the road surface

Always expect the unexpected – traffic, pedestrians, animals, potholes, and changes in the road surface

Be conscious of making the right gear selection – not so much torque as to cause the transmission to constantly snatch, and not so little as to have no power to hand when you need it

Know your limitations – if you are unsure about a particular situation, stop and evaluate the terrain or obstacle before continuing

Slow down before you get to a bad patch of road, and then gently accelerate through – by not slowing down in the first place you risk carrying too much speed as you come through the difficult area

As with any obstacle, preparation is key and practice makes perfect

SIMON SAYS...

- Always maintain control of the bike whilst getting on or off
- It's OK to use the sidestand, but never rely on it
- Always try to be on firm terrain
- Get off where it's comfortable and then walk with the bike to park it if needed

This might at first seem to be a simple thing to do, but it's definitely not something that should be taken for granted. It is, in fact, one of the most critical skills to get right. Get it wrong and you'll be faced with the prospect of lifting a loaded adventure bike back on to its wheels, which isn't the easiest of jobs.

Both mounting and dismounting from the bike requires thought. Is the bike stable? Are you balanced? Can you maintain control whilst getting on or off a heavy bike?

Never rely on the side-stand to provide stability, as it can be fatal if the bike is already loaded and the suspension is compressed. With your additional weight you may not be able to retract the side-stand without tipping the bike in the opposite direction. Ideally, you should apply full front brake, turn the handlebars to full opposite lock and lift the bike to vertical. In this position you have triangulated and locked the bike so that it cannot move as you mount.

Dismounts must be made on firm terrain. Can you get a foot down to give you stability? Is the ground firm enough for the stand? Can you remount again easily? If not, simply drive forward a few feet until you can. If you stop on a camber, remember to put the correct foot down. Sometimes it is easier to get off on a pavement and then walk the bike to a parking spot, so be clear about exactly where you want to stop. Why park your bike in a particular spot that is tricky when perhaps just a few feet

either way can make a real difference? A simple stop can be difficult for someone with a shorter inseam. Sliding on to your right buttock or thigh allows your left foot to reach the ground while your right foot can still apply the rear brake. Restarting is quite simple as your thigh will support you until you can sit squarely on the saddle.

The 'rolling mount' will only work with bikes equipped with a centre-stand. The rider mounts the bike whilst it is on the centre-stand, keeping weight on the rear wheel. Start the bike, clutch in, and select first gear. When you're ready to move off, simply lean forward to the point where the bike rolls off the stand, then gently let out the clutch and ride away. The 'standing mount' is harder and requires confidence to execute it properly. The rider stands on the left-hand side of the bike holding clutch and throttle as normal. Clutch in, select first gear then put your left foot on the left peg. Once you are balanced, de-clutch slowly to start the bike moving and 'scoot' with your right foot until you have sufficient speed to maintain balance enough to swing your right leg over the saddle as you might a bicycle.

The standing dismount is executed in reverse order, with the rider hopping off just before the bike comes to rest. Also, think about walking the bike a few feet to a more comfortable position. Once you have found the right place to stop, keep a hand on the brake for added stability and look to stabilise the bike by locking the handlebars.

How to mount the bike

1

Stabilise the bike by holding full front brake and applying full left lock

2

Mount the bike whilst maintaining stability

3

Choose your line, straighten the bars and drive off

© Robert Wicks

Riding Techniques

Balance and manoeuvrability

9

When you condense the important aspects of adventure riding, it essentially comes down to balance and control. Keep your bike upright and in line, and even the heaviest machine will feel light and nimble. If you lose the balance, the bike instantly becomes heavy, so the trick is getting the bike back in balance quickly. Many riders actually ride 'out of balance' and wonder why they feel so tired after a day's ride.

From the outset, you should take time to understand where the point of balance is for your bike. A simple exercise can easily demonstrate this, but be sure to have a friend on hand before you try it. With the bike on its side-stand, approach it from the opposite side. Pull it towards you until it is vertical. Notice how little effort is required to hold it there? Here's where your friend comes into the picture. Very carefully, let the bike fall a little to one side or the other – not so far that it hits the ground though. Be aware of just how much more effort is required to stop the bike from falling, the further away from vertical it is. Return the bike to vertical and hold it at the point of balance; now try to walk around the bike. This is fairly simple as long as you keep the bike relatively vertical where it is easy to recover from a slight tip.

Once you have gained confidence and are aware of the effect of balance on the bike it becomes simple to do. Try to do the same with luggage on board to see what effect it has on the bike's balance characteristics. What you should find is that the balance point isn't changed when the bike

is loaded, but the effort required to prevent a tip over is increased. Remembering the earlier discussion of the effects of centre of gravity will illustrate how this impacts on the bike's ride characteristics and how it is likely to respond on rough terrain.

The key to controlling an adventure bike is using your body weight to make the machine do what you want, not the other way around. If you are tense and tight on the bike, your mass is added to the weight of the bike, and when something happens you've got nothing to fight back with. By being loose and, ideally, by standing on the pegs you can let the bike move about under you, giving you the freedom to use your body's influence when necessary.

With a road bike the rider and bike are one package, but adventure bikes are different in that the bike and rider work independently of one another. With undulating terrain, the bike is constantly trying to go out of line, and needs your input to address balance and manoeuvrability. A key turning point will come in your riding when you begin to understand the importance of foot peg pressure and how it helps to address balance. When you start to use this technique and 'dance' on the foot pegs, you'll stop wasting valuable energy. Until this point you are fighting all the time to get the bike back in line.

Use your weight and input to maximise control and minimise fatigue at all times. A good example of this is when attempting to execute a 180° turn. It's best to find a wide spot on the trail with some slope. Turn the bike

Good body position maximises control on difficult terrain

📷 Touratech

↓ Try to keep your feet evenly placed on the footrest
📷 Robert Wicks

↓↓ Ensure you are well balanced before trying this!
📷 Thorvaldur Orn Kristmundsson

→ 'U' turns on the trail are inevitable
📷 Thorvaldur Orn Kristmundsson

through 90° under its own power but then let the bike roll back down the slope using the force of gravity, saving on energy by using the weight of the bike to move you into the next part of the manoeuvre. Control the roll with your brake and then accelerate forward – a simple execution that does not tire you and leaves you in complete control.

The other key element to maintaining balance is to moderate your speed. Riding a heavy adventure bike in rough terrain is not about speed, and no matter what you think your bike is capable of, the sheer weight is just waiting for the next ditch or rut to toss you to the ground. Remember that things happen more quickly at speed and if you can't stop before an obstacle ahead, you're riding too fast. Momentum certainly helps to keep a bike upright, and many riders use speed to maintain momentum and sustain their balance, thereby effectively masking their poor balancing skills.

SIMON SAYS...

- Balance and control are the two most important things
- Use your body weight to make the machine do what you want
- Understand the importance of foot peg pressure
- Always moderate your speed

Turning on the trail

1

Break your turn up into sections

2

Use the camber to help roll the bike backwards

3

Turn back to follow the right direction

© Thorvaldur Örn Kristmundsson

SIMON SAYS...

- Think of the clutch as your safety switch
- The clutch will give 'instant' control
- Make sure the clutch is adjusted correctly
- Use just two fingers to grip the lever

Clutch control

10

The clutch is an often-overlooked control on a motorcycle, and it is far more versatile than might first be apparent. The effective use of the clutch comes from knowing what it can do; for example, how it can control the amount of power delivered to the rear wheel, how you can modulate that power to find the grip point of the tyre, and how you can control a momentary rear wheel spin and restore drive.

'Think of the clutch as your safety switch,' says Simon Pavey. He adds: 'In the event of a momentary loss of control, by dipping the clutch everything calms down, you get time to regain control, get yourself together and move on. I nip the clutch all the time when I ride as I find it takes the pressure off – you feel like you're controlling the bike, not the other way round.'

By using the clutch the rider can determine precisely how much power is transmitted to the rear wheel, which is invaluable in certain conditions. Slipping the clutch during an ascent allows the engine to develop sufficient power to climb, but prevents the wheel spinning and losing traction, thus allowing forward progress. Also, slipping the clutch can prevent too much power getting to the rear wheel, keeping the front wheel down and allowing controlled and measured upward progress. If you find yourself with unwanted wheelspin, it's often better to keep a steady throttle and momentarily 'dip' the clutch to allow the wheel to bite and find grip, rather than easing off the gas.

Steady throttle is obviously essential when riding, but controlling the bike by using the throttle alone means the bike is unlikely to react as quickly, whereas use of the clutch gives far more instant control.

It's important to be able to 'feel' what the clutch is doing, so it's best to wear thinner gloves if possible. Try also to control the clutch with just two fingers, keeping the thumb, ring and little fingers gripping the handlebar – this allows you to keep a firm grip on the handlebar whilst at the same time leaving the other fingers to control the clutch, and keeping you in control of the bike.

It's also vital to make sure that the clutch is adjusted correctly and has the right amount of free play in the cable. If there isn't any, there's a very good chance that the clutch will slip when you least want it to, which will cause it to overheat and slip even more, possibly also causing permanent damage to the clutch by warping the steel plates.

A good exercise is to ride the bike as slowly as possible, but see just how slowly you can go by slipping the clutch and modulating the throttle. Once you're confident doing that, try using the brakes to come to a momentary but full stop without putting your feet down, then snapping back into balance by releasing the brake and restoring drive with the clutch. When going slow off-road, being in total control is crucial. These three items are key, and you'll need to use them like never before when riding off-road.

← **Delicate clutch control with a firm grip on the bars**

📷 Tim Cheetham

Slipping the clutch

1

Approach the manoeuvre at the right speed

2

Slip the clutch to maintain control during the manoeuvre

3

Slip the clutch to maintain drive on the climb out

📷 Robert Wicks

Braking action The use of:	Result This action affects:
Defensive Riding. Looking far ahead, anticipating problems and choosing the best line through traffic and around bad road surfaces	Your position relative to the problem area
The front brake	The front wheel and front/back weight distribution
The rear brake	The rear wheel
Snapping off the throttle	The rear wheel
Changing to a lower gear	The rear wheel

Generally one thinks of braking a motorcycle by using only the brakes, but strictly speaking this is not true. Braking is achieved by a combination of actions from the table opposite.

One is tempted to overlook the last two in the table, but both of them are quite able to lock up the rear wheel just long enough to cause the back to slide out when the bike is leaning over into a corner. Therefore, safe, confident braking on a motorbike is not a simple skill but requires practice and training, as the condition of the road surface plays a vital role.

With this in mind, consider that several factors can have an influence on your braking – from the type of terrain you are travelling across, the type and quality of your tyres, the weight of your bike, the speed you are travelling at, and the size and condition of your bike's brake discs and pads.

The front brake is always going to provide at least 70% of your braking power. Particularly in the off-road context, the rear brake should simply be regarded as a rudder to keep the bike in line, rather than relying upon it for any effective level of stopping power.

The secret of good braking on poor surfaces is observation. If you know what's under your wheels you can tailor your braking to the surface. You must brake in plenty of time, preferably while upright and in a straight line (any braking while leaned over on gravel can be extremely hazardous). Use the brakes progressively, and carefully interpret the noise and feedback from the front

and rear tyres while braking to detect and counteract any wheel lock-up, and take particular care when braking on gradients, inclines, and heavy cambers. Remember that a tyre will only offer grip and steering control when it's turning.

You should always keep two fingers on the brake lever at all times – this helps reaction time and leaves the other fingers on your right hand to hold on to the handlebars. Fewer fingers on the brake lever also means you are less likely to brake as hard as you might by grabbing the lever with four fingers. Always remember the value of engine braking as you gear down, and build this into your calculations as you plan to slow or stop. Your braking should be planned and timed for the situation at hand. You must be able to assess the condition of the road surface throughout your stopping distance, as your braking distance is very much affected by the surface.

A gentle application of pressure will result in a weight transfer, the suspension will compress smoothly, as will the tyre which then starts to bite. This added downward pressure means that you can now brake harder on the front brake with little chance of it locking up (on a good surface). As the bike dips down on to its front suspension do not stiffen your arms and prop your body up using the handlebars. Instead grip the bike harder with your legs and keep your arms loose and relaxed. If you continue to squeeze the lever, the tyre will bite in

← **Even two fingers can stop you surprisingly quickly**
📷 Tim Cheetham

⬇ **The rear wheel will lock easily on loose surfaces**
📷 Robert Wicks

- ■ **The secret to good braking on poor surfaces is observation**
- ■ **Only use two fingers on the front brake level and don't lock-up the front wheel**
- ■ **Always use engine braking to help you slow down**
- ■ **Quickly modify your body position in the event of an emergency stop**

further until a point when the wheel will actually lock. If you are conscious of what may happen and the application has been smooth, you should have time to deal with the lock-up, and the effect will be less dramatic. If, however, you snatch at the brakes, the chances of the wheels locking are far greater, and this may come with no warning. Remember that the tyre can only grip when it is turning – a locked wheel can neither steer nor brake. It's also important to note that if the suspension is moving up and down as a result of erratic braking technique, your ability to corner smoothly will be greatly affected.

The most effective point at which the brake is working is just before the wheel locks up. In normal day-to-day riding, you are unlikely to ever go to the point of locking, but it is important to know where this point is on different types of terrain. This will really only come with experience and practice and will vary from bike to bike. When the wheel does lock, it is not necessarily an instant disaster – but what is happening to the wheel needs to be recognised, and then you need to do something about it by releasing pressure on the brake lever.

The rear brake can be used to steer the bike and can be applied for brake slide turns, but its use needs to be both planned and deliberate. When it does lock up, you will probably find yourself negotiating a steep descent. It's not uncommon for inexperienced riders to panic, grab the brakes in the hope that this will stop or at least slow the rate of descent, but on a large adventure bike with significant weight behind you, this is not easy to do. The most important thing is not to get panicky, and to use the engine-braking and retain your composure as you descend. If you do find yourself panic-braking, the mistake was in all likelihood made long before the panic set in, so think and plan ahead for all braking.

The bike is generally at its most stable when driving forward slowly, so braking in an unstable environment, such as over rough or loose terrain, is not sensible – do your braking before it gets tricky, then as you start to cross technical terrain you can afford to be gently driving through. This gives you a margin for error, if needed, and it is unlikely you will ever need to brake hard if you follow this approach.

If you are forced into a situation where you must brake hard, you need to prepare your body for the effect of the braking. Whether you are sitting or standing, try in

the time available to move your weight backwards a little, get your elbows and arms up, and brace yourself for the moment the braking forces kick in. You are going to be forced forwards and you need to be ready to deal with this by modifying your body position.

In the event of having to execute an emergency stop, avoid locking the wheels under any circumstances, as this can spell disaster. Use a combination of both the front and rear brakes. If you find yourself losing grip, ease off on the brakes gently and alter your body position by moving your hips backwards.

The latest generation of ABS is fine to leave active for general riding, but for faster, more active riding, or on very steep descents, you may indeed want to deactivate the ABS system in order to get closer to the wheel-locking point than the ABS will allow; but this should only be done if you are an experienced rider.

↑ **Use both brakes for maximum deceleration and control**
📷 Robert Wicks

← **Make a difficult descent easier using a slow controlled approach**
📷 Robert Wicks

Braking on descents

Trail-brake the rear wheel for stability

Maximum braking effect comes just before lock-up

Release the brakes gently to regain traction and drive

SIMON SAYS...

- Remember you are the one controlling the bike
- Use your clutch to moderate your speed and maintain your balance
- Always use subtle inputs on the brakes
- Always be conscious of where you are placing the front wheel

Riding at low speed is much more difficult than it is at higher speeds, because at low speed the bike reacts more sensitively to its primary inputs – the steering, throttle, and brake – and it calls for practice to gain the required skill and sense of balance that you will need if you find yourself, for instance, having to ride slowly in traffic, or wanting to make a U-turn, or negotiate an obstacle or obstruction in your path.

There are a few tricks you can use to help you maintain balance while riding at low speed, but always remember that it should be you controlling the bike, not the other way round, and the correct use of the clutch, throttle, and brake is essential. Keeping a relaxed and steady body position, either seated (with your knees tucked in) or standing, will also help you maintain balance at slow speed.

The most useful tool is the clutch – it can moderate your speed and help balance, but needs to be used with finesse for the best results. If you want to generate just an extra mile an hour, get this by using the clutch, not the throttle. You can maintain a very slow speed simply by slipping the clutch instead of letting it out all the way. However, it's important to be aware that this can cause excessive wear on the clutch.

You can use the rear brake along with the throttle to help you keep the bike upright when travelling at very low speed, especially while turning. Dragging the rear brake

← **Slow speed balance is all in the hips and legs**
📷 Dennis Kavish

←← **A tricky descent needs to be approached with caution**
📷 Touratech

works well, but always remember to use subtle inputs on all the controls to maintain your slow speed.

Finally, always be conscious of both wheels when moving at slow speed. The front wheel is by far the more important and you need to be careful where you place it – hitting even a small rock at slow speed can quickly throw you off balance. The rear wheel will cope a lot more easily, but be aware of where it is going as it obviously turns inside the line of the front wheel.

The most important thing you can do is to practise until it becomes second nature. Like anything else, practice makes perfect.

↓ **Body position and good throttle control make this difficult crossing look easy!**
📷 Thorvaldur Orn Kristmundsson

SIMON SAYS...

- ■ Steer decisively and proactively
- ■ Choose a line that opens up your view of the road
- ■ The 'natural' line is not always the safest or most practical
- ■ Always be conscious of where you are placing the front wheel

Choosing the right line

13

If you have taken a motorcycle training course you will have been told to 'look where you want to go'. This has even more importance than ever when you ride off-road. Traction and surface conditions can change in an instant, and the width of the area you may need to ride through can also change rapidly. 'The key is to take a visual "snapshot" of the trail in front of you, but to then move your focal point of vision out at least 50 feet,' says Jim Hyde. He adds: 'If you fix your vision on an obstacle in the trail, you will probably hit it! Look instead at the line you want to follow, and magically you will miss the obstacle, following your chosen path.' It sounds too good to be true, but it works.

The three basic principles of choosing the right line are:
- To steer your motorcycle decisively and proactively.
- To choose a line that opens up your view of the road ahead.
- To steer clear of potential danger areas, such as the opposing lane.

You will generally be faced with two situations where choosing the right line is vital – on slower, technical parts of a trail where the presence of obstacles such as rocks or potholes block your line, or on faster, more open trails where choosing the right line helps to keep you safe and allows you to flow through corners.

← Make sure your bike's not too wide for the gap!
📷 F J Maré

On most trails there is quite often going to be a 'natural line' that develops, particularly if it's a well-used track. Many of these are made by 4x4 vehicles or trucks, and what you see at first doesn't necessarily mean it is the right line. Tracks can change over time and are subject to washaways and erosion, so be sure of your line as you ride and always look for good traction, even over rougher terrain. The corrugated surface of roads tends to peter out towards the edge where they may offer a smoother ride, so use this to your advantage.

As you pick your way across difficult terrain, be most conscious of where you place the front wheel, being sure to avoid any obstacles. Stand up for maximum visibility and constantly think one step ahead. Remember you only need a line as wide as your tyres (but allow space for your panniers).

← Be sure to look well forward and assess the terrain
📷 Touratech

The correct line

1

Moderate your speed over the uneven surface

2

Avoid wheelspin by using delicate throttle control

3

📷 Touratech

Standing up through this tricky section might have helped to identify an easier line

Many of the principles that apply to normal road riding are just as relevant for cornering off-road. Ideally, you should be able to take the line you want, make smooth progress without braking and be able to react to any potential hazards. Braking mid-corner, running wide, deviating from your preferred line, or losing traction, are all symptoms of poor cornering technique.

Arguably, the biggest risk when cornering off-road is that your front tyre will wash out as you turn. This is generally caused by too much weight applied on the inside of the turn with the result that the front tyre cannot provide enough grip to keep both rider and bike upright. Consequently, your weight needs to be equalised on either side, and the easiest way to do this is to transfer weight using the foot pegs.

Before making the turn, though, you must anticipate what is required for the corner. You need to reduce speed early enough, using the front brake well before the apex of the corner, pick the line you want, and set yourself up so you are in the best possible position to drive smoothly though the corner. Think ahead and try to take a line that will set you up for the next corner.

As you approach the corner, make the appropriate gear selection for the situation and, ideally, stick with it. Use

Cornering

14

SIMON SAYS...

- Keep your weight balanced using the foot pegs
- Drive smoothly through the corner
- Set yourself up wide to give yourself a choice of lines on exit
- Maintain a speed in relation to the amount of visible track in front of you

a higher gear (low revs and smart clutch control) rather than a lower gear (more power, high revs, and potentially some wheel spin) when you corner. Clutch control is all-important, particularly in technical corners.

If you think of cornering as simply a change of direction, then arguably a significant amount of control will come from your hips and feet. Apply pressure to the inside foot peg to initiate the turn and lean the bike to steer. Once you have committed to your intended line and established the turn by leaning the bike, you then need to switch your weight to the outside to keep balance. Move your weight to the outside peg partly through foot peg pressure but

also by keeping your outside elbow up. This allows you to adopt a body position over the outside peg and with the right weight balance. The other elbow should be reasonably straight, but not locked, and you should be looking through the corner to the line of the exit. Your outside leg can be moved away from the tank to get the maximum amount of weight on the outside. If you are seated when taking the corner, bring your weight forward and, if necessary, lower your inside leg from the foot peg as a counterbalance.

The limit will come when you have no more weight to transfer in order to counterbalance the bike. As you

↑ **Different lines, but identical body position and technique, with both riders looking 'through' the corner**

📷 Thorvaldur Orn Kristmundsson

exit the corner, your acceleration should be smooth and progressive. Transfer your weight back to help with traction and look ahead to the next corner.

The physics of turning doesn't change that much with speed so you can learn the basics at slow speed and then apply this out on the trail.

On tight corners, always approach the corner with the same thing in mind and set yourself up wide to give you a choice of different lines when you exit. Approaching the corner wide gives you the best view of what may be around the next corner and, most important, more options if you have to deal with something coming the opposite way.

On blind corners you need to minimise the risk of any oncoming traffic by approaching the corner slowly, keeping a margin if the corner tightens or a hazard appears unexpectedly. In these situations, always maintain a speed that is in relation to the amount of visible track ahead of you. What you cannot see, you cannot avoid – and if you are going too fast when you do see it, you will be in trouble.

↓A sweeping open turn is a joy to ride
📷 Touratech

Wide entry – Optimal visibility, wide choice of exit options
Tight entry – Restricted visibility, wide choice of exit options
Late entry – Reasonable visibility, limited choice of exit options

Thorvaldur Örn Kristmundsson

A steep climb can be one of the toughest challenges faced on an adventure motorcycle, so before starting off, study the ascent carefully (a small pair of binoculars would come in very handy here). Look for obstacles such as rocks and trees, or anything else that may affect your momentum up the climb. Getting half way up with the bike stalling and falling down on top of you is not what you're trying to achieve, and recovery from a hill can also waste a lot of time and energy.

Ultimately, getting up a steep incline successfully depends on the preparation you make before starting out. If you are entirely happy with the decision, you need to be fully focused, committed, and certain that a combination

← **A perfect climb!**
📷 Touratech

→ **Forward body weight keeps the rear wheel driving and the front wheel steering.**
📷 Thorvaldur Orn Kristmundsson

of your own skill, the bike, and the surface leaves the odds stacked in your favour.

Ideally, you also need to know something about what awaits you at the top. Making a steep climb only to reach the top and find there is no place to stop or turn the bike or, worse still, be faced with a steep drop on the other side is worth avoiding.

In setting up for a hill, the most important thing is to look ahead. From the bottom of the hill, pick a point at the top to look at and position your body for the climb. Once you are committed, head for your chosen line, pick a suitable gear, increase the revs through steady throttle control, and move into the power band as you take to

SIMON SAYS...

- Stay focused and commit to the climb
- Ensure you know what awaits you at the top
- Maintain drive, control and momentum
- Always try to keep the rear wheel 'hooked-up' to gain maximum traction

the climb. The bike will accelerate, but moderate it to a suitable speed. Drive, control, and momentum are vital throughout the climb. You need to quickly recognise the amount of drive available and modulate the throttle and clutch accordingly.

If necessary, stand up and move your weight forward over the front wheel. For a short, quick incline you can remain seated, but for a longer climb it's best to stand up on the foot pegs and move your weight as far forward on the bike as possible. This will lower the centre of gravity and make the bike easier to control as you climb. With your hips in front of the pegs, weighting the front wheel gives you steering control and drives the rear wheel into the ground for additional traction.

Always be careful not to rest your weight down on to the handlebars as this can prevent you from steering effectively. Keep the revs a little below the power band. Ease off the throttle if you have to, and if the bike's revs

begin to drop, ease the throttle open. Maintaining this balance should give you the necessary momentum to reach the top. Control and smoothness are key for this technique. Slip the clutch to avoid stalling, and keep the tyre 'hooked-up', always trying to gain maximum traction, and therefore momentum, as you make the climb. You don't want the back wheel to spin and lose traction, so if the revs continue to drop, simply change to a lower gear.

If the climb has been successful, remember it is best not to power up over the lip as you will have little chance of stopping if there is a huge drop on the other side – something which can be quite common when riding in sand dunes.

One final point to note is that if you are riding in a group, particularly one with mixed skill levels, it's best for any steep ascent to be made individually – if one rider goes down, anyone riding close behind may find their path blocked and likely to suffer the same fate.

←An ideal body position for a climb
📷 BMW Motorrad

⬇Always look for the best grip during a hard climb
📷 Dennis Kavish

Adventure Riding Techniques

If you make it halfway up the hill but find yourself running out of momentum you need to act quickly and decisively to save the situation. There are two likely scenarios – you come to a natural stop and remain on the bike. This is quite possible, especially if the track is clear of obstacles and ruts. If this is the case then there is a simple technique involved to get you going. The second scenario is the more complex one where you have actually come off the bike having either run out of speed or you have crashed as a result of an obstacle.

In the first instance, if you are still in control, come to a complete stop, putting your left foot down and use your right foot to hold the bike on the rear brake. Turn the handlebars to the left and gently release the rear brake to let the bike slowly roll backwards and to the left. When the bike can't roll any further back apply full brakes front and rear and start turning the handlebars from side to side. This movement of the front wheel will let it slip slowly down the hill-face. Once the front wheel is below the rear and, ideally, at about 45° to the face you can think about releasing the brakes and slowly rolling back down the hill. Descend carefully, get your breath back and, before you attempt to retake the hill, work out what caused the problem at the first attempt.

In the second case, where you cannot control the situation and you see that you are going to stall on a

← **Assess the climb before you go too far…!**
📷 Andy Turk

section that is too steep, it may well be time for you to part company with the bike. Jump – ideally, sideways and as far as you can within reason. If you must go down, try to fall into the hill, as falling the other way (off the side of the hill) can have dire consequences. Allow the motorcycle to fall down and away from you – a controlled fall is always better than an uncontrolled one.

In this instance, you always know you are not going to make it before you run out of momentum, but many riders will try to reach the top of the climb even when all is lost. You need to recognise when this point comes and deal with it. Going beyond the point is not at all sensible.

← **Even the best of us lose it sometimes!**
📷 Thorvaldur Orn Kristmundsson

Recovering the bike

1

Oops!

2

Turn the bars to full opposite lock

3

Use the handlebars as a lever and lift from the end

- **React quickly to what is going on**
- **Assess the situation before making any decisions on recovery**
- **Rotate the bike using its extremities**
- **Always stay uphill of the bike**

If you do go down on the hill, get your breath back and, if you've fallen hard, check for any injuries. Only then should you begin to assess the situation. If your wheels are facing uphill, the bike needs to be turned around with the wheels facing downhill. You will lose a considerable amount of energy and may even incur an injury by trying to pick the bike up if it is in this position. Keep the bike in gear at all times and stay off it – making a mistake sat on the bike could be costly and you may end up falling down the hill as you panic after the crash.

Look at the ground and decide which way is best to move the bike around. Use the bike's extremities, such as the front wheel, for maximum leverage. This will also help to conserve your energy. Pay close attention to your brake and clutch levers, which can easily get caught and snap off as you rotate the bike.

Carry out this manoeuvre patiently, working the bike round to a lateral point on the hill with the wheels on the lower side. This will make the bike much easier to pick up. Lock the handlebars, get a solid footing on the slope, and then pick the bike up. Use your thigh to rest the bike on if you cannot get it up in a single movement. Once the bike is upright, twist the handlebars backwards and forwards to the full lock position – this will help to bring the front wheel of the bike round and facing down. You can also use the biting point on the clutch to let the bike roll around to the point where you run out of gravity. The use of gravity will also help to conserve energy. Not until the front wheel is sufficiently far round (at least 45° to the hillside), and you are happy with the escape route, can you even think about getting back on.

It's essential to stay uphill of the bike. Trying to get on from ground that is lower than the bike is dangerous, as the bike can easily fall back on to you. Once on, you can further improve your angle with additional sideways twists of the handlebars. When sufficiently round, check your escape route again and proceed down the hill. If you have any doubts, or are injured, it is best to walk the bike down the hill, controlling the speed of the descent with the front brake and clutch.

If necessary support the bike with your thigh

Continue to lift to a stable position

Assess which way you need to steer out

Use the camber to help roll the bike back

Let gravity help you roll the bike forward to an escape route

Always stay uphill of the bike, remount and off you go!

Steep descents on any bike can certainly be intimidating, particularly over loose gravel or if the surface is slippery. Add the weight of an adventure bike with luggage and it takes on a whole new dimension. The entire manoeuvre takes commitment, confidence, and a belief that the bike can get you down in one piece. Vitally important is the ability to maintain steering control of the motorcycle at all times, and to make the most of what grip is available.

As you start the descent, you will feel the motorcycle 'plunge' down the first few feet, but quite quickly its speed will level out as the engine braking kicks in. The

→ **The new Tenere
is a competent
lightweight
overlander**
📷 Yamaha

SIMON SAYS...

- **Maintain steering control at all times**
- **Use engine braking to exploit the available grip**
- **Don't grab the front brake**
- **Stay easy and relaxed through the descent**

Steep descents

effect of engine braking should not be underestimated, but it takes confidence to rely solely on this throughout the descent if the surface is very loose.

It's unlikely you will move out of first gear during the descent, though this is largely dependent on the gradient and how comfortable you feel. Remember that despite moving slowly and not applying the throttle, the bike should not stall unless you stop.

A combination of delicate brake input and making the most of the engine braking will allow you to exploit what grip is available. The traction itself is really a function of the

type of terrain interacting with the tyre and the amount of force pushing the two together. Braking will transfer weight to the front wheel and away from the rear wheel.

There is always a temptation to grab the front brake hard in an attempt to slow your rate of descent, but doing this is likely to result in locking the front wheel and going down in a heap. The front brake should be applied gently, and this is best done using two fingers (index and middle fingers together). You will soon feel the point at which too much brake is being applied and

Hill descent

1

Approach any descent
with caution

2

Assess the route
before committing

3

Be prepared to negotiate
obstacles or steps

how quickly the front starts to lock-up and slide.

It is also easy to lock-up the rear wheel and thereby lose any stopping power as you trundle down the hill. The rear brake is best used to help transfer weight to the front.

A common mistake is to come up over the top of a hill to start a descent without realising just how steep the drop is and immediately grab a handful of front brake. The front wheel locks and all control is lost in a second. If this happens, it's important to ease off the brake quickly and allow the tyre to regain grip. An easy application of the brake is key to a successful descent. By gradually

loading the chassis and wheel, the braking effect will be maximised and this should make it easier to stop with less chance of sliding.

As you navigate your way down, keep your arms easy and relaxed, and grip the bike with your knees when the need arises. Try to move your weight backwards as far as possible, especially your hips, to allow your legs to take more weight. This should mean less fatigue as you descend.

Look ahead to the end of the descent and prepare to deal with the upcoming terrain, which could be anything from an intersection to a jump or a ditch.

📷 Greg Baker

4

Constantly reassess and check your route

5

Consistent and steady braking is the key

6

Plan your exit and drive through

Riding in ruts is possibly one of the hardest techniques to master properly. Shallow, muddy ruts can be a nightmare, with the front wheel slipping around making balance hard to achieve – even worse if the front and rear wheels end up in different ruts. This is one occasion where you need to put weight on the front wheel, giving good grip and steering, and keeping it planted in the rut. Standing up is best, but not if it is at the expense of crashing. Remember the basics – balance on the foot pegs, maintain a clear vision, use a high gear and drive forward. If you panic and shut the throttle, it's likely you will crash by losing the front, so maintain your forward momentum through smooth throttle control. This way the rear wheel should provide sufficient drive to maintain forward progress without the front washing out. If the ruts are deep, then try to keep your feet in close to the bike to prevent them dragging or getting caught on the side of the rut, and as a last resort there's no shame in 'paddling' along with your feet. This technique may, in fact, help to conserve some energy.

When your feet are on the foot pegs, remember to move them slightly backwards so that if you hit something your foot just gets knocked off, rather than getting caught underneath a rock or other obstacle. Doing this will allow you a little more finesse on the foot pegs if needed. The best way of dealing with a rut, however, is to avoid it, so look for another route around the rutted section.

Crossing ruts and other obstacles requires a completely different technique. You should always evaluate the obstacle if you are uncertain. If you feel confident, then it is imperative to try to cross the ruts as squarely as possible with the bike upright. There's a great danger that an angled approach will let the wheel drop into the rut and sweep the front end from underneath you.

The correct technique requires quite an aggressive approach, with the body pushed backwards weighting the rear wheel. This, combined with a good twist on the throttle, should be enough to ease weight on the front wheel and let it 'float' over the rut while the rear provides the drive to get across. Once you're over, ease back on

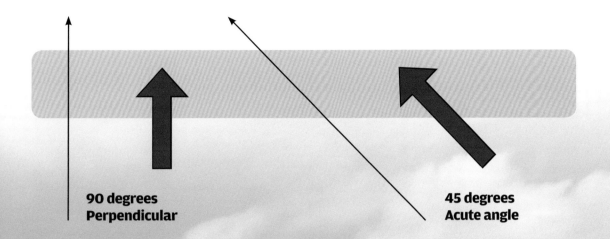

**90 degrees
Perpendicular**

**45 degrees
Acute angle**

the gas and resume the forward attack position to regain maximum steering response. Tree roots and other such obstacles require a similar technique, differing only in that you should try to get as much weight as possible forward as soon as you're over the root to relieve pressure on the rear wheel, allowing it to roll over the obstacle.

A ditch requires a fair degree of confidence and ability. Again, approach it aggressively, but use a squirt of throttle sufficient to lift the front wheel as you approach the lip of the ditch. If executed properly, the front wheel should land on the other side of the ditch, and the bike's forward momentum should be sufficient to drag the rear wheel

← Looking at the right route!

📷 Adam Lewis

↑ Take every opportunity to improve your chance of success!

📷 Joe Pichler

back up over the lip of the ditch. If there is any doubt that the ditch is traversable or that you have insufficient skill to get over, then it is prudent to try to find an alternative crossing or to simply walk the bike over the ditch.

There will doubtless be a time when you will encounter a step or drop. Climbing a step is not easy and should only be attempted if you are confident of success. It requires a high level of skill, timing, and courage. Assess the height of the step, anything greater than 20–25in (50–60cm) will be difficult to clear on an adventure bike and another route should be found. If it is feasible, however, a slow, controlled approach in the attack position should be made perpendicular to the step, with the bike in the upright

position. Your objective is to lift the front wheel using throttle and clutch just high enough to allow it to clear the step.

The 'wheelie' should be started a few feet away from the climb, which will allow you to gain sufficient momentum for the rear wheel to climb up the step. In this elevated position you must attempt to put as much weight as you can on the front end as the bike hits the lip of the step. If you get it right, the bike's bash-plate will hit the lip and the bike will effectively pivot around that point, planting the front wheel back on the upper level. Your forward momentum should be sufficient to allow the rear wheel to bite into the upward face of the step and drive up and forward on to the upper level. Breathe a sigh of relief and proceed.

Tackling a drop is slightly easier but still requires a high level of skill and commitment. If the drop isn't so steep that you'd hit the bash-plate on the lip, then it's probably best to approach it as you would a steep descent, with your body mass pushed back, less weight on the front wheel and allowing the bike to simply roll over the step. If the drop is more significant, a different technique is required. The objective in this instance is to land on two wheels, which will spread the impact of landing and make it easier to control the ride away.

Assess the drop, if at all possible, to make sure there are no surprises waiting at the bottom. A perpendicular approach is essential to maintain control on landing. At a few feet from the lip enough throttle should be applied to completely unweight the front wheel. If the manoeuvre is completed properly, the motorcycle will remain in a horizontal attitude as the rear wheel continues to drive forward. The bike's momentum will carry it forward over the drop to land squarely on both wheels.

It should be noted that these techniques can have a relatively high impact and will apply high levels of force and load to the motorcycle which might result in stress cracks or fractures in chassis or pannier frames. Consider the feasibility of removing luggage before attempting such manoeuvres.

↑**Sometimes it's better not to stop!**
📷 Chris Smith/ Liz Peel

↓**Which way would you go?**
📷 Dennis Kavish

■ **Left side –** Well travelled but with unknown water hazards
■ **Middle –** Direct but bordered by deep ruts
■ **Right side –** Initial rut crossing followed by smooth run

Sand recovery

Assess your position, look for firmer ground

Pull the wheel onto firmer terrain

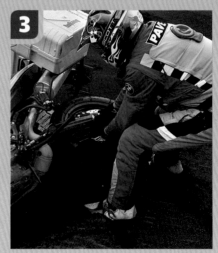

Stabilise the bike

At some point on your travels you are going to run into trouble. With the exception of component failure, the most likely problems are getting bogged down in mud or sand, getting stuck in a land feature, or drowning the engine during a water crossing. Some are easily resolved, but others might require a bit of thought to sort out. What follows is by no means an exhaustive list, but by their nature adventure riders tend to be a resourceful bunch and usually find a way out of trouble.

Sand or mud

The most common situation you'll encounter will probably be finding yourself with the rear wheel stuck axle deep after trying to find grip in soft going. Spinning the wheel merely makes the situation worse by digging you in deeper. Mud saps energy from the rider and power from the engine as both struggle to find grip. Once you have stopped, take a second to gather yourself and decide what to do. If the going is particularly poor it may be necessary to remove some luggage to lighten the load on the rear wheel and help stop it sinking further. Stand astride the bike with both feet on the ground taking your body weight. If this is not possible, then stand to one side of the bike ensuring that you can control both throttle and clutch. With the engine running, keep a steady throttle and modulate the clutch, letting the bike rock forwards and backwards in the rut. Eventually you'll build sufficient rhythm and momentum to allow the bike to climb out of

the hole and drive forward. Keep your speed going until you've reached firmer ground and can remount. If you need to enlist help, then make sure they push only as the machine is driving forward.

Being stuck in sand requires a slightly different extraction technique. You'll have most likely come to a halt trying to drive through a soft patch, with the rear wheel dug deep into the sand. Again, consider the feasibility of removing luggage to reduce the rear wheel weight, as the recovery requires a degree of lifting. The technique involves pushing the bike over on to its side so that the buried wheel is lifted up out of the sand. Once it's free you can fill the hole up with sand, but stamp it down as hard as you can to compact it enough to support the bike's weight. If the sand is still too soft, then add some brushwood or foliage (if there's any around), or even your jacket or other garment, to give the tyre the purchase and grip required to drive out over the soft sand. To prevent the front wheel digging in once you're on the move you'll need to put your weight as far back as possible and use plenty of throttle to keep the front end light. When you're on a firmer surface, stop and return to collect anything you left behind.

Land features

You might find yourself riding along a ravine out of which there's no obvious easy exit, nor any room to turn round. Here you face the prospect of having to manhandle the bike up and out over the ravine edge. There's no easy way,

← **Walk the bike under power to a firmer surface**
📷 Thorvaldur Orn Kristmundsson

Use the handlebars as a lever

Lift the bike into position

Apply opposite lock and remount

just brute force and ropes if you've got them. The principal concern must always be the safety and security of the people concerned in the operation, so care must be taken at all times. If there's no possibility of lifting the bike out, then consider using the same technique to lift the bike up on to its rear wheel, then pivot it 180° and drop it back on to two wheels and drive out.

Water crossings

The single biggest risk attached to water crossing is the danger of completely submerging the bike, effectively 'drowning' it. If this happens, water will be sucked into the inlets and possibly into the cylinder itself. The engine will stop immediately, but hopefully without damage. Recovery will be difficult, so care must be taken to not fall victim to the current. Once the bike is back on dry land you can start the process of removing the water from the engine. Water is not compressible, and if any volume remains in the cylinder while it's turned over there's a very good chance that you'll bend a con-rod, effectively crippling the engine. Never under any circumstances crank the engine, either with the kick-start or the starter motor, until you've removed the spark plug. Check the air-filter element – if it has got wet, then it will need to be removed and dried. Check the spark plug and dry it if necessary.

Once this is done, the motor can be cranked to blow any water out of the cylinder. If using the kick-start, give it at least 50 very vigorous cycles, or at least 30 seconds

Man handling the bike

1

Try to get the bike as far as possible under its own power

2

Enlist all the help you can ...

3

... to pull the bike onto level ground

continuous cranking on the starter motor. Once you are confident that all the water is out of the cylinder, refit the spark plug and air-filter and attempt to restart the motor. With luck the engine will cough back into life and you can get back on the road. If it doesn't start, then water has got into the electrics and they will need to be dried out. You may have to remove the tank to gain access to the ignition coils, but in any event you will need to spray with WD40, or similar moisture displacer, any wiring or cabling you can see that is wet. A quick squirt down the plug hole and into the plug cap won't go amiss and will aid the drying out process. If no mechanical damage has been done, then the engine should start. It is wise to let the engine idle for a few minutes, but check that there's no significant amount of water in the oil. If there is a lot of water in the oil, then you can attempt to drain it off by tipping the bike to one side and letting excess water drain out of the filler hole. If the gearbox is free of water then you can continue, but check the oil filler cap after

a few miles – if water has seriously contaminated the oil then you'll see a milky-coloured paste inside the cap, and possibly also inside the oil tank or cam cover. If this is the case, then you must change the engine oil at the earliest opportunity to minimise the risk of oil starvation and consequent damage to the engine.

Punctures

These are an unpredictable hazard and you can ride a thousand miles and not get one, yet riding through an area of acacia trees can give you four or five in as many miles. Whilst initially daunting, there's nothing too difficult about fixing a puncture once you've done a couple. A dry run at home is a good idea, and if your bike doesn't have a centre stand, work out how to support it, perhaps with a pannier under the sump, or a log under the rear footrest, for example. Be comfortable with removing the wheel, and how to break the tyre's bead from the wheel rim. Don't forget to keep your puncture repair kit easily accessible.

↑ **Practice and a handy prop make this tyre change look easy!**
📷 Touratech

↖ **Waterproof boots are a sensible option!**
📷 Danny Burroughs

↓ **It's surprising what you can achieve by the roadside!**
📷 Metal Mule

↑ **This is the easiest way to pick up fuel**
📷 Touratech

Running out of fuel

This is something nobody wants to do, especially if you're a lone rider in a remote area. Your planning phase should have identified fuel stops, so you will be able to estimate how far away the next fuel point will be. If it's a reasonable distance, and you're comfortable with leaving the bike unattended for a few hours, then get walking. You'll find someone with a truck in the next village who'll be able to find fuel and take you back. Other than that you'll probably have to wait it out and flag down the next vehicle to go by. Generally people will stop and offer help.

Roadside repairs

Maintenance on the side of the road is something that all overlanders will have to tackle at some time or other, but it's impossible to predict exactly what might go wrong. Whatever the problem, though, don't be afraid to have a go at fixing it – if it's already broken it's unlikely you're going to make it any worse! A broken pannier rack could be temporarily fixed with a stick inside the two halves of the tube and an overwrapping of duct tape. A cracked or holed crankcase could be patched up with J-B Weld. A blown fuse can be bypassed with a single strand of wire, but only once you've found out why it's blowing.

Picking the bike up

1

An unplanned manoeuvre

2

Take a moment to assess the situation

3

Take a firm grip on the end of the handlebar

Picking the bike up

Dropping your bike is something that you hope never to do, but it is an eventuality that none of us will avoid. It's not the end of the world, but getting the bike the right way up again can be a bit of a struggle – unless you know the easy way!

First and foremost, always take a breather before starting. You'll probably be mad at yourself for dropping it in the first place, but you'll also probably be quite tired. Never rush at it and try to pick it up from the side – you are very likely to pull a muscle in your stomach or damage your back. Take a moment to assess the situation and prepare yourself as well as the area around the motorcycle, which should be clear of obstacles.

Make sure you've enough room to manoeuvre yourself as well as the bike. If the bike is on its right side, then engage first gear to lock the rear wheel, preventing it from rolling during the lift, if it's on its left side, then hold the front brake on. Turn the handlebars to full lock, to the left if it's on its left side and vice-versa for the right side. Deploy the side-stand if possible. Remove excess luggage if necessary.

Method 1: Facing the bike, squat down and cup your hands underneath the end of the handlebar where you can get maximum leverage. The bars should be at full lock. Keeping your back straight in the classic lifting

position, keep your arms straight and start the lift using only your leg muscles to raise the bike. If you have the strength to complete the lift, do so, otherwise you can prop the bike on your thigh until you can get it up fully.

Method 2: Face away from the bike and squat down so that your bum is backed up against the saddle. Reach behind you and take hold of the handlebar with one hand and the rear grab rail with the other. Straighten your arms and start to 'walk' backwards using the power in your thigh muscles to do the lifting. Be careful not to over-lift and dump the bike on the other side, otherwise you'll be doing it all over again!

⬆ **This lift might have been easier without luggage**
📷 Chris Smith/ Liz Peel

Use this point of maximum leverage

Start to lift the bike upright

📷 Robert Wicks

Use your knee and thigh as a prop if necessary

Chapter 5

Specialist techniques

Thorvaldur Orn Kristmundsson

The more you ride, the greater the range of challenges you will face. With a sound understanding of the essential skills described in the previous chapter, you will be well equipped to tackle almost anything that comes your way. But as you master the core techniques, you will soon want to start pushing the envelope a little further, and this is where the specialist techniques come in handy. From riding at speed, to jumps and brake slide turns, this chapter outlines the main specialist skills that, once mastered, will take your riding to the next level.

You're likely to do yourself an injury if you attempt any of these techniques without a sound understanding of the essential skills that underpin your riding. Adopt a cautious approach when starting out and, ideally, attend a professional training school to perfect the various techniques in a controlled environment. You'll be amazed at just how quickly you scale the learning curve.

Once you can confidently counter-steer the bike as you accelerate out of a power slide, or feel completely comfortable riding at high speed, adventure riding takes on a whole new dimension. You find yourself riding with more confidence, getting further in less time, and tackling challenges you had previously never contemplated. ■

- **The Attack position makes you much more responsive**
- **Try to keep your weight central**
- **Look forward to where you are going, don't fixate in front**
- **Enjoy the ride!**

Riding at speed is fun to do. It is exhilarating and it is dangerous, and there are few better exponents of the technique than those top-level riders who take part in the Dakar Rally. It will take you some time to gain sufficient experience to ride at speed with confidence, and it's always worth remembering that adventure riding is about going far, not necessarily fast.

As with most of the more advanced techniques described in this book, it will come naturally as your skill level develops, but if you are desperately trying to ride fast without the requisite skill levels to cope with things when they go wrong, the consequences can be serious, so it's best to let the skill and technique come naturally.

You need to be standing up for maximum visibility with your body in what is best described as the 'high speed attack position'. This means your body needs to be forward of the neutral position – this aids visibility, adds weight to the front of the bike to keep it stable (most important if you hit something at speed) and helps with balance with the increased wind blowing against you. A firm grip on the handlebars is necessary for added stability. Remember that riding at speed means everything comes at you quickly, and things happen a lot faster, so your reactions will need to be very quick.

It is essential to be in complete control of the bike at high speed and to match that speed to the conditions – it's not possible to ride at the same speed over rocks or through sand as you might on a gravel road. For sand

← Volcanic
sand pistes in
Iceland are a
joy to ride fast
📷 Thorvaldur Orn
Kristmundsson

↑ Riding doesn't
get any better
than this!
📷 Touratech

Riding in sand at speed

1

Try to stay flexible as you hit a soft surface

2

Be prepared for the bike to move around beneath you

3

Keep your head up and elbows bent

←←**The attack position gives good stability and forward vision.**

📷 Waldo van der Waal

↓Snow does not offer much in terms of grip and traction!

📷 Thorvaldur Orn Kristmundsson

riding, you need to move your weight further back on the bike and maintain a firm grip on the bars, as the front end will move about in the loose substance. With this in mind, you should ride within your limits, as a high-speed crash generally results in a serious amount of damage to both rider and bike. Never be overconfident, as things can rapidly get out of hand. To stay in control you need to think well ahead – your observation skills and vision are critical – and as your speed increases you must think and look even further ahead.

Various things, one of which is trying to navigate while you ride, can adversely affect your level of control over the bike, and your focus on the road ahead. Repeatedly scanning the terrain and then looking down at a GPS or other instrument is a challenging task and a skill in its own right. Rally-raid riders travelling at high speed against the clock naturally ease off the power just before looking down at their road books to give themselves a small margin in the event of unexpectedly confronting something.

It is vital to be vigilant and alert at all times, looking for animals, ruts, potholes, and other hazards. Use the safest route possible to avoid obstacles, constantly modifying your line to keep progress as smooth as possible.

Riding at speed is physically demanding, and good upper-body strength is called for to maintain this for long periods and to bring the bike back in line should it be deflected by striking an obstacle. In such an event, it will help to keep the throttle open.

It is unlikely that you will be able to maintain a fast pace over rough terrain for long periods, so be sure to slow down, and even stop, if you are feeling tired. If you press on when tired there's every chance you will have an accident.

📷 Thorvaldur Orn Kristmundsson

4

Try to keep your weight as far back as possible

5

Confident use of the throttle keeps the front end light ...

6

... letting you power over the soft sand

- Approach the turn in a low gear from the forward attack position
- Leaning forward weights the front wheel and maintains steering
- Use the rear brake hard to flick the bike round at the apex of the turn
- Past the apex release the brake and power out of the turn

Brake slide turn

1

Approach the turn at a good speed

2

Begin the turn, weighting the outer footpeg

3

Transfer weight forward before applying rear brake

Brake slide turns

21

The brake slide turn has its origins at the motocross and enduro track where the manoeuvre is often used by riders to set themselves up for the inside line in a turn, allowing them to sneak underneath the rider in front. The movement shortens the corner and/or lengthens the following straight. Only use this technique on slow, sharp corners that have no ruts or obstacles.

This is not really a manoeuvre well suited to the big trail bike, and in an adventure riding context it should only really be used to change direction in tight situations or to turn quickly where there is limited space.

To practise brake sliding, first try going at a moderate speed down a smooth track and just locking up the rear wheel. Get used to this feeling and then gradually use your body, either in the seated or standing position, to coax the rear end to the left or to the right as the bike slows down – you may find yourself twisting your body to accomplish this. There is no need to exaggerate the move, just do it several times, increasing each time the amount you twist to get the desired effect.

Although not extremely difficult to perform, the slide must be timed so that you finish with all the sideways motion and begin accelerating before you usually would had you followed the normal arc of the turn. You want to stand the bike back up as soon as possible so you'll be on the widest part of the tyre, which will allow you to use the most throttle without sliding out.

In essence, as you approach the point of the turn, the

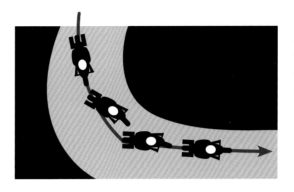

← **Steer into the corner as the rear wheel steps out**

dynamics mean the motorcycle will want to continue in a relatively straight line, so the exercise needs quite a bit of input from the rider. You have to commit, and you need effort from your hips to move the bike into the turn, especially with a large adventure bike (much less so with a smaller machine).

Your body position should be far forward on the bike to get more weight over the front wheel to make it stick, and less weight over the rear to help it move out as you brake and initiate the slide. As you apply the brake your body will move forwards naturally.

Vision is fundamental, as is the need to set up early as you approach the point of execution. Think about what you are trying to achieve and remember that the slide and resulting skid mark is not an arc – it is more like a 'tick' shape, where the energy of the turn dissipates in the last second and the actual change of direction comes right at the end of the manoeuvre.

As you approach the corner, pull in your clutch and place a lot of pressure on the rear brake. As you enter the turn, the rear wheel must lock and stay locked in order to make the turn. If you don't keep it locked, the outcome is either an unpleasant high-side, or it may simply roll out. Steer the bike to the inside of the corner, leaning in as you do so. Applying pressure to the inside foot peg will result in the rear wheel sliding away. Too much pressure and it will break away more. Applying pressure to the outside foot peg will result in the tyre biting in – the tyre will grip more and the bike will straighten up. The rear wheel should slip free of the dirt's hold and slide towards the outside of the corner. These movements pretty much all happen at once and cause the motorcycle to turn the corner more sharply. As you pass the apex of the corner, begin to let out the clutch and ease on to the gas again.

Only once the bike is stable and upright should you consider getting on the power. It's essential to feel what the bike is doing and not just to rely on the power as you complete the movement.

← **A well executed brake slide turn is a dramatic manoeuvre**
📷 Thorvaldur Orn Kristmundsson

4

📷 Thorvaldur Orn Kristmundsson

Braking hard on the apex will kick the rear wheel out

- ■ **Approach the turn confidently on a slightly wide line**
- ■ **Initiate wheel spin as you approach the apex of the turn**
- ■ **Weight the outside peg and counter steer to control the slide**
- ■ **Balance throttle and steering to maintain your line**

The power slide essentially uses the throttle to spin the rear tyre to make a sharper corner. The technique allows you to accelerate fast in a long sweeping corner – it may look easy but requires practice to perfect. It is used to great effect by professional riders on both the motocross track and in rally-raid events. It's even something you will see from time to time being used by MotoGP and Superbike riders as they drive out of a corner. Power sliding, as strange as it may sound, is about losing control while still being in control.

In terms of technique, enter a slow first or second gear bend that is free of ruts or obstacles. Pull in the clutch slightly as you approach the apex of the bend, and then increase the amount of throttle while releasing the clutch rather abruptly. This will cause the rear wheel to spin as the bike exits the apex, with the result that the bike performs a sharper corner.

Power slides

22

You need to understand that the rear wheel will no longer be in line with the front wheel. The front wheel will be pointed forwards while the rear drifts to the outside. It is at this point that you need to exercise considerable care, as you can either fall prey to a low-side or, worse, high-side the motorcycle and end up in a heap on the side of the road. In a high-side you're ejected from the bike. In a low-side, the rear tyre loses traction and you end up sliding with the bike on the ground – the only consolation being that it tends to hurt less than a high-side.

To practise power sliding, a useful starting point is to find an open piece of flat, firm dirt and do 'doughnuts' over and over (one foot on the ground and let the bike spin pivot around you). Keep doing them so you get a feel for how the rear tyre breaks away from the grip of the dirt and spins free. Then practise cornering near two tyres set 60ft apart. Stick to second gear and ride around them cornering only at the point the tyres are placed.

Start slowly and build up speed progressively. Ride in a clockwise direction and do not use any brakes for this exercise. The point is to feel how your rear tyre starts to lose traction as the motorcycle's handlebars are dipped into a corner. As you enter the corner it is important to move forward on the bike – this will help to govern how much weight is placed on the rear wheel, and therefore the traction it can generate. Be ready for the rear wheel to misbehave – it will occasionally break loose and try to turn the bike through 180°. To prevent this, transfer more weight on to the outside foot peg, or learn to counter steer – the act of turning the handlebars in the opposite direction you are moving in. For example, while cornering left, the left handlebar grip is pushed forward and the right grip is pulled back. As your experience builds, your hands will react instinctively in a corner.

⬇ Powersliding is an exhilarating way to take a long bend
📷 KTM

Steering with throttle

1

Setting up your approach
on a slightly wide line...

2

... allows you to steer
into the turn ...

3

... as you open
the throttle ...

In power sliding you will notice that the more throttle you apply, the more the rear tyre will spin and want to break away. Expert riders can run fast in wide sweeping corners because they have the skill to use a balance of power and steering input to see them through the turn.

The amount of slide that can be generated will depend on the terrain. Loose surfaces, like sand or gravel, make power sliding easier. You will have mastered the technique when you find yourself sideways, yet you're still accelerating out of the corners. It's that 'out of control but still in control' moment you're striving for. Once you have mastered power sliding, try the technique standing up. It's a little more challenging as you cannot use your foot mid-corner for support, and success really depends on your ability to control the slide by applying different amounts of weight on the inside foot peg.

← **Steve Hague executes this power slide with deceptive ease!**
📷 Robert Wicks

← **Controlling wheelspin is the key to success**
📷 Robert Wicks

... spinning up the rear wheel ...

... as you power through the turn

📷 Thorvaldur Örn Kristmundsson

- Use minimal throttle to prevent slipping down the camber
- Weight the outside peg to push the bike into the camber
- Be aware that sudden pressure on either wheel will help to push the tyre sideways down the hill
- Use positive camber to your advantage wherever you can

The camber of a road is essentially the difference in elevation between the two edges, otherwise described as the inclination of a road's surface. This can be as simple as a track or path cut into the side of a hill, or an engineered road surface with a high central crown and lower kerbs or edges. Riding on any camber requires caution, but especially on unmade road surfaces, so care and planning must be exercised.

You should always try to use the camber to your advantage. Positive camber will help to hold your wheels in the turn by offering more traction. You seemingly have the ability to go faster through the bend than if it were flat, and it can be fun to do. Here, centrifugal force (the one that works in a Wall of Death stunt) takes over from gravity as the dominant force. While the bike is leaning as normal to take the corner, the actual angle of lean in respect to the road surface is quite small. In these circumstances grip and traction become secondary considerations as the camber effectively 'holds' you in the turn, and one often gets the sensation of a 'slingshot' as you exit the turn.

By contrast, a negative, or off camber corner is one that slopes the other way, forcing you to take the corner slower than if it were flat. Straight away grip and traction are compromised as there is a risk that over application of throttle or brake could send the wheel skating down the slope. You turn through the corner feeling that the

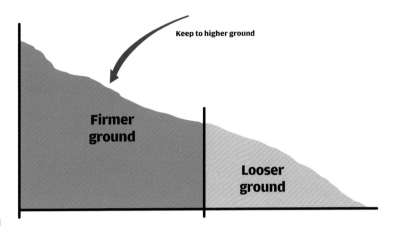

Keep to higher ground

Firmer ground

Looser ground

front wheel could go at any time. Off-cambers are tricky enough, but add an ascending or descending slope, plus muddy or loose gravel, to the equation and it can get really challenging. Putting as much weight as you can on the outside footrest shifts the centre of gravity further to that side, effectively pushing the wheels into the hillside. Getting it wrong by bearing on the inside peg will simply transfer more weight to the inside, increasing the tendency for the wheels to slip away from the road.

Imagine you are attempting a steep descent, with an off-camber situation thrown in for good measure. First and foremost is line selection and, quite often, riding higher up the slope gives you more margin for error. (Though this is not always the case, the ground higher up may be firmer

← **Bodyweight and balance are critical factors when riding off camber**
📷 Thorvaldur Orn Kristmundsson

Negative camber

1

Delicate throttle control and weighting the footrest on the low side ...

2

... helps prevent the rear wheel slipping down the camber ...

3

... allowing you to safely negotiate the slope

📷 Thorvaldur Orn Kristmundsson

– a visual inspection will give you an idea of what you are dealing with.) Adopt the same body position as if you were approaching a flat corner. It should be outside the line of the bike with your weight on the downhill foot peg. This helps the tyre to grip, but it's a delicate balance because as soon as you transfer too much weight to the outside, the bike tries to tip over and down the camber. You need, therefore, to counterbalance the effect of the weight by keeping your outside elbow bent up – this will help to tip the bike and maintain a comfortable position. Sustained forward vision and good gear selection are essential, as are very gentle touches on the controls. A sudden application of the throttle or brake can have a significant impact.

Allow the wheels to roll, but have a feel for what is going on because any sudden pressure on either wheel will help to push the tyre sideways down the hill. Once again there is a balance to be found – it's good to carry some momentum, but ultimately a slow, steady pace is what you need, as the slower you go the less force there is acting on the bike to pull it sideways.

Positive camber, on the other hand, can be a real advantage if used correctly. Take a banked corner, for example. What changes is that the positive camber effectively gives you ground to work with, and additional traction, allowing you to accelerate around the bend and take the long way round the corner – much as you might see motocross riders taking a corner. To do this successfully, you need to commit to get round the bend quickly. Move your body weight to the front of the bike, and on to the outside peg, and try to flow through the turn. Remember to look ahead and draw an imaginary smooth-flowing line through the turn as you exit. Accelerate smoothly out of the turn, keeping your body forward for front-end traction and control. Carrying more speed allows you to lean with the bike and slingshot out. It is a safe technique to use, as you are generally using the flat part of the tyre as you enter, run through, and exit the turn. If you're not comfortable with this it may be easier to take a tighter, more conventional inside line.

A final point on camber that everyone should be aware of is that many gravel roads have natural camber on both sides created by a man-made crown – the slope of a road surface to the outside being to aid drainage. Excessive road crown creates either a positive or off-camber situation depending on whether you are turning left or right.

Assume you are riding on the left-hand side of a road with a crown that drops away to either side of the centre line. If the road bends round to the left, you have positive camber and can look to take the bend with confidence. If, however, the road goes round a right-hand bend you have an off-camber situation and need to proceed with caution. During long stretches on quiet roads, it's easy to lose your concentration, and some riders get into the habit of using both sides of the road to take advantage of the camber. You need to be extremely careful doing this in case there is someone coming the other way and you find yourself having to return to the other side of the road and being forced to deal with an unexpected

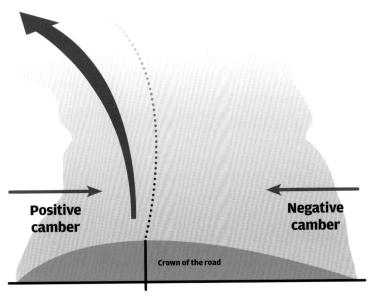

off-camber situation. Your weight and body position will be wrong for the situation, you're likely to be carrying too much speed, and it can be difficult to correct, with the likely result of you ending up on the other side of the road in the bushes at best.

SIMON SAYS...

- ■ **Know what you're jumping into!**
- ■ **Approach your jump as squarely as possible**
- ■ **Use enough throttle to keep the front wheel up as you take off**
- ■ **Keep the front wheel straight to prevent a wobble as you land**

Executing a jump on an off-road bike can be one of the most amazing – and scariest – feelings in the world. Ideally, jumps are best avoided on a fully-laden adventure bike because the suspension and chassis are already carrying a heavy load and don't need to be coping with the extra impact. Enduro and motocross bikes are designed to handle jumps – they are lightweight machines and, more often than not, by simply getting the power on they tend to correct. Their heavyweight race equivalents – rally race bikes like those that compete in the Dakar Rally – are much heavier but have excellent suspension and a better spread of weight. A heavily laden adventure bike, by contrast, generally has too much weight in the wrong places, and going sideways off a jump can be extremely difficult to correct, and the suspension is not capable of dealing with the momentum of the weight going the wrong way.

That said, if you find the opportunity, why not ditch the luggage and have some fun.

Thorvaldur Orn Kristmundsson

The following are the key things to remember when it comes to jumps:

- When approaching the jump it's important to be in the standing position, to choose a good line and the correct gear.
- It's essential not to launch at an odd angle which could kick the rear out or send you off to the side.
- Use of the throttle should be smooth and even, accelerating slightly as you leave the upslope, ideally from a smooth spot.
- If you accelerate too much it is likely the front of the bike will lift as you launch. If this happens, it is essential to transfer your weight to counteract this by leaning forward. Pulling the clutch in and tapping the rear brake can also assist in pulling the front of the bike down.
- If you ease off the throttle as you launch, the front wheel will fall forward and send you into a nose dive with scary consequences. To raise the front of the bike, get the rear wheel spinning as fast as you can by accelerating in the air. This technique helps but has limited impact, particularly if it is a steep dive.

↑ **Steve Hague shows just what a big bike can do!**
📷 Robert Wicks

- Always look ahead towards where you are going to land and beyond.
- On landing, use your legs to help absorb the impact and ensure your shoulders, arms, and wrists are in line with the front forks. This spreads the pressure evenly through your arms, chest, and shoulders, and won't damage your wrists.
- Let the suspension compress and rebound naturally.
- Always accelerate just before landing. This will help to maintain your momentum on landing by directing the bike in a straight line. This is particularly important in rutted and uneven terrain.
- If, during the jump, the bike moves sideways in the air, it's best not to panic. Concentrate on keeping your body in line with the front suspension and accelerate on landing.
- Whenever possible, check the jump and landing areas before you attempt it. Having an idea of the line, speed, and landing can make all the difference between a successful jump and a nasty crash.
- Do not attempt a jump if you are not confident of success.

Dakar: The ultimate adventure riders

If ever you want to see some of the best motorcycle control and technique on show, look no further than the participants in the infamous Dakar Rally. Widely regarded as the toughest off-road challenge in the world, the Dakar Rally started back in 1977 when Thierry Sabine got lost on his motorcycle in the Libyan desert during a race from Abidjan to Nice. He returned to France knowing that he had been defeated by the dunes, but promised himself that he would share this experience with as many people as possible.

Between 250 and 300 motorcycles take to the start line, and the competitors face significant challenges designed to test their abilities over varying types of terrain, and always against the clock.

The rally demands preparation at many levels – physical, technical, and motivational. More than a simple race, the Dakar requires outstanding off-road navigation capabilities, rock solid consistency, and the highest level of technical performance from the rider if he or she is to make it to the finish line.

← **The Dakar Rally offers every terrain imaginable in the world's toughest off-road race**
📷 KTM

→ A purpose
built rally bike
handles these
conditions
with ease
📷 KTM

→ Man and
machine in
perfect harmony
📷 KTM

With speeds consistently well above the 100mph mark, terrain which varies from massive sand dunes, river crossings, camel grass and rocks, and a multitude of hazards including stray animals and pedestrians, riders in the Dakar need focus, commitment, and skill. Furthermore, with extremely long sections, some of which can run to 600 miles and more in a day, endurance, motivation, and physical fitness are vital – even the smallest mistake can be very costly. Riders are pushed to the limit in every respect, and sleep deprivation is a reality from the outset. Add to this the physical demands of racing at speed across rough terrain and one can begin to appreciate the rigours of this event.

Technical specifications
KTM 690 Rally bike

Engine

Engine Type	Single cylinder, 4-stroke
Displacement	654cc
Bore x Stroke	102mm x 80mm
Compression ratio	11.5:1
Maximum torque	69.5Nm/6,000rpm
Performance	approx. 70hp/7,500rpm
Starter	Electric
Transmission	6 gears
Carburettor	Keihin FCR 41
Control	4V/OHC
Lubrication	Pressure lubrication with 2 oil pumps
Primary ratio	36:79
Final drive	X-ring 5/8in x 1/4in
Cooling	Liquid cooled
Clutch	Wet multi-disc clutch, operated hydraulically
Ignition	Kokusan DC-GP 93-59

Chassis

Frame	Chromium molybdenum, power coated
Front suspension	WP USD 52 MA
Rear suspension	WP-Monoshock
Suspension travel front/rear	300mm/310mm
Front brakes	Disc brake 300mm
Rear brakes	Disc brake 220mm
Front/rear rims	1.6 x 21in/2.5 x 18in
Front/rear tyres	90/90-21in/140/90-18in
Transmission ratio	16:44
Battery	12V/8Ah
Wheelbase	1,510mm
Ground clearance (unloaded)	320mm
Seat height (unloaded)	980mm
Fuel capacity	approx. 36 litres
Weight	approx. 162kg

➔ **KTM's rally bikes have dominated the Dakar for many years**
📷 KTM

📷 Joe Pichler

Riding off-road over long distances is both physically and technically demanding. To ride with confidence and stay in control, you need a combination of motivation, strength, endurance, flexibility, rapid reflexes, and good coordination. Some of this will come simply through application of the correct technique, but there are a number of other contributing factors that will aid your comfort, safety, and enjoyment. From following simple guidelines when it comes to nutrition and hydration, to thinking about your own personal safety, planning your route, first aid, and dealing with cultural differences, this chapter gives you insight into a host of things many of us often forget to consider in any depth but which can all have a bearing on our riding and what we gain from the experience.

Whilst technique won't save you from the inevitable, you can at least take steps to minimise the risks inherent in exploring the wide world. As a novice traveller you will experience cultures and attitudes that are new to you, and you will see things that are a million miles from our Western 'comfort zone'. Children demanding money or presents will flock to you like moths to a candle, and men and women, very often appearing as if from nowhere, will pester you to buy their wares. You will meet people who will be willing to share what little they have with you, and you will come across children whose greeting is a stone thrown at you as you pass.

What is certain is that you will be exposed to risk and danger throughout your travels. In some cases it will be blindingly obvious, in others more subtle and insidious, and it is how you manage and prepare for this that ultimately determines the extent of their impact on you. ■

Motivation and mental preparation

Adventure motorcycling appeals to people for different reasons – some head off to fulfil a lifelong dream, others to convey a message to the world, while many use it simply to get away from the rat race. Whatever the motivation, appreciate that you will be confronted with a number of mental and physical challenges, particularly on trips of longer duration. Your mind plays a huge role in how you ride – your mood, concentration, and thoughts have a big influence – either positive or negative, and in the end there is no magic recipe of personal traits to suit an overland adventure, but there are a couple of key factors to consider:

Attitude – Start small by doing an initial trip over a long weekend, then extend this to a week the next time round to assess if you are happy with what it will take to sustain this type of activity over a longer period of time, further from home and over tougher terrain.

Mental toughness – This is not the Dakar Rally, but at times it may feel like it, and at times you may be extending yourself further than you thought possible. This is the ability to control your own mind and remain both positive and focused no matter what happens.

Being alone for long stretches – Even if not on a solo trip, one gets a lot of time to think.

Determination – It is important to have the end goal in sight at all times.

Concentration – Maintaining concentration will greatly assist in a smooth ride and being alert to possible dangers.

Flexibility – It is vital to be prepared to adapt, as your detailed plan just could pale into insignificance when out on the road.

Positive thinking – Before starting a steep climb or crossing a deep river, imagine yourself doing it perfectly. Fill your mind with the right picture, and often the body will follow through. Think negatively and you may well fall off.

Fitness – Riding a fully-laden adventure bike for long stretches is a physically demanding exercise and you will need a reasonable level of basic fitness to cope with the demands.

← **You will need to be prepared for riding in almost any type of conditions**
📷 Touratech

↑ **Focus and determination always help**
📷 Thorvaldur Orn Kristmundsson

↓ **Riding on this sort of stuff can be tricky so a good level of fitness is useful**
📷 Thorvaldur Orn Kristmundsson

↑ You certainly get time to think when you're out on the road

📷 Chris Smith/ Liz Peel

Ultimately your mindset for adventure riding comprises:

- Your understanding of your ability to handle the bike you are riding.
- Your understanding of your bike's ability to handle the terrain you are heading into.
- Your ability to read the terrain in front of you.

Jim Hyde says: 'When you plan to take an off-road adventure trip, your skills are the determining factor for where you can go. You need to be confident in your abilities (whatever their level), you need to have practised with your motorcycle so that you are aware of its

capabilities at your current riding level, and you need to use common sense to keep yourself within your personal limits.'

He adds: 'Mindset equates in many ways to commitment – the commitment to "just do it". You can't be timid on a big bike. Like when you are going up a steep hill, you have to hit the throttle and go because momentum is your friend in situations like that, but you have to commit, you can't say to yourself "we'll see how it's going when I'm halfway up". That simply won't work and you will not make it to the top. You need to say to yourself "I'm going to go full bore and I'm going to make it!" You also need to be able to "see" yourself on the other side of any obstacles, and that is what mindset is all about.'

Physical fitness

By Rodney Womack

Regardless of the type of riding that you do, physical fitness plays a big part in the enjoyment of the activity. Whether you are riding for pleasure, adventure, or competition, being physically fit will make a huge difference in the way that you feel during and after the ride. And, your enjoyment level will go up as your overall fitness improves.

When it comes to adventure riding, increasing your strength and conditioning should be a priority before you ever get on the motorcycle. Improving your fitness will not only increase the enjoyment of riding, but it is also important in the areas of safety, controlling the bike, and negotiating through difficult terrain. Increasing your strength will make handling a heavy bike much easier, while improving your overall conditioning will help make the long distances in the saddle much more manageable. Your recovery time after a long day on the trail or road will also be accelerated when you maximise your fitness.

But, what is the best approach to improving my fitness before I hit the road?

The first choice is to train at home with basic bodyweight exercises such as squats, push-ups, pull-ups, sit-ups, lunges, and the jumping rope. These types of exercise require little or no equipment and are quite easy to get started with. They are also quite capable of building impressive strength and endurance for whatever activity that you take part in. In addition to the strength-building exercises it is always a good idea to add some general conditioning work such as walking, jogging, cycling, swimming, rowing, or any other similar type of activity that will get your heart pumping and improve your overall fitness.

The other alternative for building strength to handle the stresses of adventure riding is through weight training. Obviously, this type of training would require you to have weights in your home or for you to join a gym with the appropriate equipment. Either way it will require you to spend some money and to get some specialised instruction in the proper methods of training.

For the purpose of the average rider, I would recommend a programme of bodyweight exercises that you can do at home. This is the best approach for the beginner, and the more advanced trainees can simply add more exercises, intensity, sets, repetitions, or time to the workouts.

The following would be a good workout for the beginner. If it proves to be too easy, simply add more sets and repetitions until you reach the level that matches your current fitness requirements.

Beginner's workout
- Jog in place for 5 minutes.
- Stretching for the upper and lower body – 5–10 minutes.
- Push-ups – 1 to 3 sets of 10–20 reps.
- Pull-ups – 1 to 3 sets of 5–10 reps (you will need access to a pull-up bar for this one).
- Sit-ups – 1 to 3 sets of 20 reps.
- Bodyweight squats – 1 to 3 sets of 10–20 reps.
- Jog, cycle, swim, rowing machine, or jumping rope (or any other endurance/aerobic activity) for 15–30 minutes.

This is a simple, but effective programme. If you struggle with any of these activities, just do what you can, and try to add a repetition or two to each workout. For those who have not exercised in a while, start with only one set of each exercise for the first week before adding more in the following weeks. It is advisable to start slowly to avoid injury before increasing the intensity of the workouts.

If the aerobic work is difficult for you, start with 10–15 minutes and add some more time at each workout. this type of simple exercise programme can be done three to four days per week. Another option, if you prefer, is to do the aerobic activities and the strength exercises on alternate days.

A simple exercise programme such as this will help you establish a good base of strength and conditioning. Just adjust the workout to your individual preferences and fitness level and you will be on your way. Once your fitness improves, then you can move on to some more advanced workouts with more resistance and intensity.

With improved fitness you will be able to ride for longer periods of time, handle your bike more effectively, ride more safely, recover faster, and, ultimately, have more fun. Improving your strength and conditioning will also improve your overall health, and, most important, it will help to prevent injuries if you do suffer an accident. When planning your next ride, it is a good idea to add strength and conditioning to your list of 'things to do'. In the end, it will make your ride much more enjoyable!

Rodney Womack is a Certified Strength and Conditioning Specialist (NSCA), a high school sports coach in the US for 20 years, and MX racer since 1971. Through his website – www. motoxfitness.com – he writes a free weekly MX fitness newsletter

Stretching
Upper and lower body for 5–10 minutes

Push-ups
1 to 3 sets of 10–20 reps

Sit-ups
1 to 3 sets of 20 reps

Pull-ups
1 to 3 sets of 5–10 reps

Squats
1 to 3 sets of 10–20 reps

Aerobic activity
15–30 minutes

Nutrition and hydration

On the road your diet is likely to be different from what you traditionally eat at home, but it is vital that you get enough of the right sort of food given the physical nature of an adventure trip and the need to be mentally aware at all times. Diet plays a major role in this respect and the right sort of nutrition will also assist in combating illness and make you less susceptible to infection. Just as your motorcycle will not run well on poor quality fuel, your own body will not perform well if any fuel source is inadequate. A common myth is that recreational riders don't need the same approach to nutrition as a professional rider – this is not true because as recreational riders we are often nowhere near as fit as professionals and therefore actually stand to benefit even more from the correct nutrition.

Equally important is leaving for your ride in good condition, and nutrition plays a fundamental part in your preparation before leaving home. The following general rules are recommended for most riders to help create a healthier regime ahead of an adventure ride. Start by trying to limit or eliminate the following from your diet:

■ Food or drinks with excessive sugar.
■ Products with white flour.
■ Fried foods.
■ Junk food/fast food.
■ Highly processed food.

Concentrate on eating a good balance of 'natural foods' such as lean meat (chicken, fish, lean beef), fresh vegetables, fresh fruits, yogurt, milk, and wholegrain cereals. Divide these foods into five or six small meals per day with a good balance between protein, carbohydrates, and fat. Taking a good multi-vitamin/mineral supplement every day is also important to ensure that your body is able to function at a high level.

For those who need to lose weight, cutting back on carbohydrates such as potatoes, bread, and pasta will help you get started. Ultimately, you have to burn more calories than you eat to lose weight. Eating less and exercising more is a good, safe means of reducing your body fat level. But, be sensible about it – don't lose more than 1–2lb per week. If you drop your calories too low, then you won't have the energy to train properly.

Everyone reacts differently to training and diet, and you may need to experiment with different foods and meal patterns before you find the combination that works best for you. You should, however, strive to create a balance in the foods and meals that you eat.

Depending on the length and nature of your journey it is probably best to take certain food items from home and purchase additional items en route from village markets, street vendors, and supermarkets. Also take the time to enjoy local cuisine – each region will undoubtedly have its own delicacies that are worth trying as part of the travel experience. Food can generally be taken in tin cans or dehydrated foil bags, and some in its natural state repackaged in an appropriate container. Tinned food comes ready to eat but does weigh a lot and can take up a lot of space. Dehydrated packs are lighter and easier to pack, but use up a lot of water when rehydrated.

Here are some useful food tips for when you are out on the road:

- Vary your intake of food to include a mixture of carbohydrates, proteins, fat, vitamins, and minerals.
- On extended trips it is worth considering taking a course of multi-vitamins and mineral supplements to ensure your body is getting what it needs, particularly if your diet may be limited or cannot easily be varied.
- Heating food sufficiently will kill bacteria.
- Avoid raw seafood and meat and also be wary of salads which are difficult to clean and are easily contaminated.
- Always try to have a stock of 'snacks' which can be eaten during rest breaks, such as dried fruit, nuts, energy bars, chocolate, boiled sweets, biscuits, and crackers.
- Follow basic hygiene rules when preparing food and always wash your hands before eating.
- Fruit and vegetables should be reasonably safe if peeled or cooked.
- Always check the 'sell by' date on tins of food before purchasing.

Hydration

Some level of dehydration is a given on any ride, and an overland journey in hot desert conditions will only exacerbate the extent to which water is lost from the body through sweating and urination. These lost fluids must be replaced, as failing to do so will result in a series of increasingly serious health issues. In a hot and arid climate it is quite possible to become heavily dehydrated in a matter of hours, and the human body can only survive for a limited period of about five days without water in a moderate climate. You will therefore need a regular supply of water, primarily for drinking, but also for washing and cooking.

Think of your body as an engine – it requires fluids to keep it cool, lubricated, and performing well. It doesn't matter what you are doing, you need water, lots of it. It is essential that you keep yourself well hydrated before, during, and after each ride if you want to maintain good performance, concentration, and control. Good hydration will also help to avoid early fatigue, the effects of which can be hugely detrimental to riding confidently off-road. Even slight dehydration can produce a serious downturn in performance through an increase in body temperature.

Consumption of water must be roughly concurrent with the loss (in other words, if you are perspiring, you should also be drinking water frequently). Drinking water beyond the needs of the body entails little risk, since the kidneys will efficiently remove any excess water through the urine with a large margin of safety.

A person's body, during an average day in a temperate climate such as that in the UK, loses approximately 2.5 litres of water. This can be through the lungs as water vapour, through the skin as sweat, or through the kidneys as urine. Some water (a less significant amount, in the absence of diarrhoea) is also lost through the bowels.

In warm or humid weather, or during heavy exertion, water loss can increase significantly through perspiration, all of which must be promptly replaced. In extreme cases it is not possible to drink enough water to stay hydrated,

↓Be sure to pack enough water for a longer trip
📷 Andrew Smith

**Tough riding
conditions will
only exacerbate
your level of
dehydration**

📷 Joe Pichler

and the only way to avoid dehydration is to reduce perspiration through rest and by moving to a cooler environment. Signs of dehydration include headaches and fatigue. Keep yourself hydrated by drinking small, frequent amounts of fluid during your riding (two or three gulps every 10–15 minutes) even when you are not thirsty.

You will continue to feel thirsty until you are completely rehydrated. Plain water, however, can actually switch off the thirst mechanism; but having the presence of sodium in the water prevents this. It's not essential to worry about the other minerals and electrolytes that are contained in commercial sports drinks. Although they are lost in sweat, there is not an immediate need for them unless you are out in more extreme (hot) environments, in which case an electrolyte drink with minerals can be a good idea.

Staying healthy on the road requires you to be vigilant about the water you drink. This includes being cautious of ice which might be added to a drink at a hotel or restaurant. Today, bottled water is widely available in many remote locations, but you should always check that the bottle is sealed and has not been tampered with (i.e. refilled with tap water before being sold). Any water which comes from the wild or is purchased on the roadside definitely needs to be filtered and purified.

Water purification is needed to remove contaminants from drinking water so that it is pure enough for human consumption. It involves getting rid of parasites, bacteria, algae, viruses, fungi, potentially toxic minerals, and man-made chemical pollutants. A water purification system is probably not necessary unless you are travelling to really remote areas and taking water from streams or wells. If you are travelling without access to reliable water sources, then any water should first be filtered to remove particles and then be purified to remove any harmful organisms.

Water is quite heavy and can take up a lot of space, but it's a resource that you cannot go without. Basic water bottles or steel fuel bottles from your local camping store will suffice. Be sure to keep them clean and, much like fuel for your motorcycle, fill up at every available opportunity. Bottles are best located inside your panniers but if you need to store them externally on the bike, make sure they are fastened securely and check on them regularly.

A lightweight hydration system (such as those made by Camelbak) is an extremely useful item. They come in different sizes and the water is easily accessible through an over-the-shoulder valve. Consider a pack which has some additional storage space as this can be used to carry essential items when heading out on day trips.

Route planning

This is where your journey starts to become a reality rather than just a dream. All those ideas, places, and things to see are connected somehow, and all you've got to do is sort out the route. Planning your journey is a vital component of any adventure ride because the last thing you want to do is get lost. This can not only cause delays, but adding extra miles to your journey can cause higher levels of fatigue and even panic if you cannot quickly resolve the quandary.

Research is essential, and whether you have a mediocre trip or an absolutely spectacular journey will depend on how well you do it. There is a growing resource of information available to the modern traveller, some relevant to motorcycle travel and some not, but anything you learn about your destination or your route will prove useful at some time or another.

The Internet is full of little nuggets of information that overlanders look for and cherish when they find them. Books such as the *Rough Guides* and *Lonely Planet* can also be very useful, providing a lot of information about towns and hotels that might be off the beaten track. Ensure that you source the latest maps and talk to fellow

travellers about their recent experiences in the area you plan to travel.

Take time to make a financial plan as well, be sure about how much cash you're likely to need based on your estimated mileage and accommodation costs, then add a contingency budget. Research your destinations to see if you can access cash, either from banks or ATM machines, to save you having to carry large amounts of currency.

Planning any journey requires a good sense of how far you or your companions can reasonably travel in one

↑ This wasn't on the map at home!
📷 Touratech

↓ Good planning and research are a must before you leave home
📷 Robert Wicks

Touratech

day, bearing in mind that this will be variable according to the terrain you expect to encounter and the time of year you will be travelling. On a good sealed road aboard a large adventure bike you can expect to be able to cover anywhere up to 500 miles (800km) on a good day, depending on your tolerance levels.

The same road on a wet and chilly day might only give you half that distance. On a well-surfaced piste, around 200 miles (320km) might be a reasonable target, but at the height of summer in the desert it may well be impossible to travel very far during the heat of the day. On poor and unpredictable tracks, especially if you expect to encounter deep sand, 100 miles (160km) in a day is a realistic expectation.

Consider also what you want to do when you arrive at your daily destinations. If you have sightseeing planned, then it's best not to be too tired to appreciate and enjoy

where you are. If you intend to set up camp somewhere, then allow yourself enough time to unpack and pitch the tent, as well as make a meal, in daylight. Use the night-time to relax and recover your energy ready for the next day.

A decent map is absolutely vital, both for planning and for the road. In your planning phase, the 'big picture' that an unfolded, large-scale map offers is second to none in visualising the route you want to take. Mount the map on a board and use pins to show any points of interest you want to see, then draw the route you intend to follow. If you can, hang it on a wall – you'll find yourself stopping to look at it every now and then, modifying routes and visualising the terrain – it's a fantastic motivator! Your adventure begins to take shape as soon as that line is on the map.

With the map marked, you can assess the terrain you're likely to encounter,

and from that get a reasonable idea of how far you'll be able to travel on any particular day. Use those points to identify towns within striking distance of your end-points, and research places to stay. While fuel will probably be readily available on most parts of your journey, it's advisable to have an idea where it might be found and plan those stops in too, not forgetting to include water on the to do list. If your journey is going to be more than can be covered by one set of tyres, consider planning a tyre stop too.

Be prepared to explore, talk to the locals, and don't be afraid to stray off the beaten track.

BMW Motorrad

↓**Stop and establish your location if you think you're lost**
📷 Chris Smith/ Liz Peel

Navigation essentials

What is navigation? Navigation can be as easy or as hard as you want it to be, but in essence it's all about knowing where you are and where you want to go. Never before has it been easier to know our position to within a few metres accuracy – modern GPS systems make it all so simple, but that's only a small part of the story. Knowing where you are in relation to somewhere else is the critical factor and one that a GPS alone cannot determine. This is where the 'old' technology of paper maps becomes useful to us once more; indeed the GPS almost takes second place.

Basic navigation skills, like being able to use a compass and read a map, should be learned and practised long before your trip starts. Take time to look at the maps of your route and visualise the contours of the terrain, the landmarks, and settlements you'll pass on the way – you'll be surprised what you recognise when you actually get there.

If you are taking a GPS receiver, then take time to learn how to use it before you start your journey, there's not a lot of good trying to program your route into it while you're on the ferry. Not all maps have been digitised for use with GPS programs, but most GPS manufacturers have their own map sets that can be quite detailed. Market leader Garmin, for example, have their 'World Map', which contains quite detailed mapping of most areas of the world. Whilst not to street level, all global major and many minor principal routes are mapped.

For those wanting to produce their own data to use with their GPS, various digitising programs are available, of which 'ExpertGPS' is a great example. Using a digitally scanned image of your map, the software overlays a latitudinal and longitudinal grid over the map image based on three known coordinates. This allows the program to interpolate a grid for the whole map from which coordinate data can then be extracted. The program has a range of features, one of which allows for data transfer to and from your GPS unit, allowing you to both create a route and upload it to the GPS unit as well as downloading and plotting your track details into 'ExpertGPS'.

Once you've uploaded your route to the GPS, stick the paper map into your map-pocket and it's as easy as following the arrows.

From a technique point of view, you need to be cautious when riding and navigating. Looking down at the map or GPS limits your vision, and choosing to do so at the wrong moment might lead to hitting something in your

path. If the terrain is rough, slow down before looking, or stop altogether, especially if there is any doubt in your mind about your location or heading. It takes great skill and control to constantly be swapping your vision between the road and the GPS or map – just ask any rider in the Dakar, and many of them will agree that this is one of the toughest challenges.

Personal safety

Adventure motorcyclists have a distinct advantage over their 4x4 counterparts in that the bike is perceived as far less a symbol of wealth than the large four-wheel equivalent. Use this to your advantage, but always maintain a common-sense approach to safety-related issues. Your personal safety is paramount, so always be vigilant and adopt the right approach if things get awkward. A smile and eye contact will often defuse a tricky situation but you should be prepared to cut your losses and run if need be. However, you are more likely to be pleasantly surprised by the hospitality and kindness offered by local people. As a general rule, though, don't at any point place convenience over your personal security. Note the following key points:

Bike – Your No. 1 consideration when staying at a hotel or campsite is safe parking for your bike. Many places that don't have obvious secure parking will often let you park inside the lobby – simply ask the manager. Irrespective of where you park, consider making use of a bike cover – it is by far one of the best security devices and you will be amazed by how 'invisible' it makes your bike. In most countries theft is not an issue, but 'fiddlers' are, and a couple of fully-loaded adventure bikes rolling into a small town are bound to attract attention.

Riding gear and equipment – Other than lugging your riding gear with you when not on the bike, one of the best security options is to make use of an adjustable, lockable wire mesh net which can either fit over the outside of a backpack or simply act as a 'hold-all' for storing your riding gear when stopping at a tourist attraction. You can fit your riding kit (including boots and helmet) into it, lock it to your bike and put the cover over whilst you walk around in more casual gear. Another useful investment is a spiral

cable lock. It can be used to secure your helmet and jacket by threading the cable through the arms and helmet visor and then to a secure point on the bike. With your bulky gear securely fastened to the bike, you can take a walk or do some shopping without having to worry. Be vigilant about your other equipment, in particular high-value items such as cameras and other electronic goods, taking them with you whenever possible or packing them in an obscure and hard-to-reach part of your luggage.

Accidents – The adventure biker's worst nightmare. The big word here is insurance – make sure your personal cover is adequate and check the small print of your policy to be sure that it covers motorcycling or any other hazardous activity you will be pursuing. If in doubt, seek the advice of a specialist insurer such as Endsleigh who specialise in 'adrenaline' pastime cover. If you are the injured party, try to contact your insurer as soon as possible to arrange either repatriation or local medical assistance. If you are unfortunate enough to injure a local person, be prepared for a world of trouble, as even the most minor injury will become life-threatening in the hope of the victim getting a large pay-out. It is essential to

remain calm, but offer help if you can. The local police will usually be involved at some stage, but use your judgement and choose a time to offer to pay for the damage or injury caused. This will usually be sufficient recompense and you can be on your way slightly poorer but much wiser. Do not expect the insurance you bought at the border to be of any use at all, but without it you will have to grease a palm or two. Wherever you can, report any accident or incident to the police as soon as possible after it has happened and insist they provide you with a report – this can be difficult in certain countries but will be useful in the event of an insurance claim.

⬆ **Make it difficult for an opportunist to undo your luggage straps**
📷 Robert Wicks

⬇ **Even a minor spill can be dangerous in the wrong place**
📷 Touratech

Bribes and payments – Bribes, however they are dressed up, are a part of Third World life. At most border crossings there will be a group of locals touting for business as 'guides' to help you through the sometimes complex customs procedures. This can be money well spent to avoid hassles and save time that would otherwise be wasted waiting in queues and walking back and forth between offices. Agree a figure before the deal is struck but expect to be pestered for more. Never surrender your passport or any other papers, but insist that you hand them to the officials yourself, and the 'helper' will stick to you like glue. When you're finally cleared it's time to pay up, but it's funny how quickly they stop being your best friend when you decline their request for double the fee you agreed! Out on the road you are more likely to encounter local police, and as a tourist you become a target. You might be stopped for a minor traffic infringement and will be asked to pay an on-the-spot fine. It is usually pointless trying to argue the toss, so again it's simpler and quicker to just pay up and move on, but don't expect a receipt!

Communications – This doesn't sound like a security consideration, but if you are travelling in a group of two or more, bike-to-bike communications is one of the best security aids you can invest in. When reading a map and trying to navigate through an overcrowded city with no discernible directions, you aren't always able to keep an eye out for the rest of your group, making it easy to get split up. Two pairs of eyes will always be better than one – if the lead driver is busy following the route prompts, the tail rider can be observing and advising of other hazards. Off the bike the single most valuable asset will be the humble mobile phone. Don't be tempted to use call-time on your own contract – it will cost a fortune! It is far cheaper to buy a pay-as-you-go SIM card from a local trader, but ask them to activate it for you, because you won't be able to follow the instructions in the native language. If you are travelling in a particularly desolate region you might consider investing in, or short-contract hiring, a satellite phone.

← Avoid carrying too many currencies by buying what you need at the border
📷 Robert Wicks / Globebusters

Money – Cash is king! Credit cards will only be accepted in larger metropolitan cities, so don't rely on always being able to use your plastic. It is best to keep a reasonable amount of local currency to hand, certainly the minimum required to cover your fuel and food expenses. Exchange facilities are usually found at the borders, but don't expect the cheapest rates. In larger towns, either use a bank or keep an eye open for ATM-style money changing machines. Making sure your cash is safe is imperative. Keep a few coins and notes in your pocket for smaller purchases, but larger amounts of cash should be kept hidden, either in your luggage or a money belt. If you are travelling somewhere where mugging might be a problem, then consider keeping a dummy wallet while secreting the bulk

of your valuables somewhere else. Keep a low profile and avoid ostentatious displays. Keep money and credit cards hidden – ideally in a money belt pouch, and be discrete when paying for goods, especially at the roadside. Be aware of pickpockets in markets and crowded streets, keep your wallet in a front pocket, never in a back pocket.

Systems – Develop systems and routines to make your life on the road simple. For example, always keep your keys in the same place when not in the bike, and keep your panniers organised, thereby making it easier to find things. Routines make unfamiliar environments seem a little more familiar, which in turn means you are less likely to forget something or expose yourself to some sort of unnecessary risk.

↓ Even in remote locations security must be considered
📷 Robert Wicks

Dealing with cultural differences

There is no magic formula to ease the transition to a new country, but there are a couple of things you can do which will certainly help. First, some research into the country you are visiting will help tremendously. Being aware of basic cultural and religious differences and making an effort to learn even a little of the local language will make a tremendous difference. This will give you not only a head start on arrival, but also immediate respect – if you show an interest in the other person's language and culture they will show an interest in you, and this can help to get things done more efficiently.

Second, always head off with an open mind and a willingness to learn – it's important to try to look beyond the stereotypes and misinformation that often exists about certain countries. Also, don't expect things to be done in the same way they are at home. Only once you have spent a period of time in a particular country can you start to make judgements of any sort. It's also important to be conscious of, and respect, local rules.

Particularly on long journeys, always be prepared to spend a few days in some of the major cities. This may provide for some real culture shocks in terms of driving habits, food, bureaucracy, and culture. Approach this with an open mind, as not only will it allow you time to secure visas, carry out repairs to the bike, change money into local currency, check e-mails and replenish both spares and essentials, like food and water, but it will offer you the chance to experience a very different way of life and to see things from a different perspective.

As a western tourist it is inevitable that at some stage you will be approached by a smiling man offering to be your guide. They will use their guile and charm in the hope that you will let them take you round the city. If you agree, you will end up in their cousin's trinket or carpet shop where an equally charming man will offer you tea and ultimately subject you to a very hard sell. To these guys you are a source of income and they can be incredibly persistent, but use your judgement, know when to say no and say it politely but firmly. If you do decide to buy something, you will be expected to haggle and negotiate for the best price.

On a final note, remember that the pace of life in Third World countries is generally much slower, and the sooner you get used to this way of working, the better. Use the opportunity to attempt to cross the bridge into a new and exciting culture – in the vast majority of cases it will be the most rewarding of experiences.

Survival techniques

If your overland trip involves travelling through more remote parts, there's the possibility that you might become stranded at some stage. Being prepared for this takes little time or effort and could well save your life.

Before you leave, try to ensure somebody knows what your plan is, what your likely route will be, and when you expect to arrive at your destination. Likewise, try to make sure that someone at your destination is expecting you, especially if you are travelling solo. If you are travelling with a second motorcycle, ensure that you are both fully aware of your route, and have in place contingency plans should either of you suffer a misfortune.

In the event of a serious problem, the first thing to do is to take stock of your situation. First and foremost it is important to remain calm and collected – panic solves nothing and simply wastes energy. You ought to have a map of the region you're travelling through, so you should know roughly where you are, and therefore you should be able to determine where the nearest settlements or roads are likely to be. After your initial appraisal there are some basics steps you must take to ensure your safety and well-being until you are rescued or recovered. The fundamental requirements are shelter, water, and nutrition.

↑ This could get tricky...
📷 Nik Boseley

→ A good fire can keep you warm, cook your food and dry your socks too!
📷 Istock

Shelter to protect you from climatic extremes, keeping you warm and out of the wind or rain, or cool and shielded from the sun. This will help to conserve energy and reduce dehydration. A tent is ideal, but a simple bivouac or tarpaulin strung from the bike will also provide cover – anything is better than nothing.

Water to keep you hydrated is essential and you should not ignore the early signs of dehydration. The importance of carrying an ample supply of water cannot be over-emphasised. Humans will only last a few days without water – so it's worth taking as much with you as possible. Remember that your intake of fluids will increase quite significantly as you get on the move.

Nutrition is last on the list of priorities as you can survive for quite a long time without food. As with water, however, resist the temptation to eat if at all possible as it might have to last you until you are picked up. Both digestion and defaecation rob you of precious hydration, so eating less can also help your water last longer.

Once these basic needs have been addressed you can assess your situation and look at your options. If you are travelling with a second motorcycle you should consider sending someone ahead to seek help, or leaving your bike and travelling pillion on the other bike. If you are travelling solo, clearly mobile or satellite phones are the simplest and most convenient methods of raising the alarm and alerting the authorities of your predicament.

It is usually best to stay put, make your presence as conspicuous as possible and wait for help. If you have access to anything that will burn, then a fire can make smoke which will be visible for many kilometres in daylight hours. Stones or clothes can be arranged in a symbol large enough to be seen from passing aircraft. At night you can use your bike's headlight as a flashing beacon that can be seen for up to 12 miles (20km).

If, however, you've no signal or sat-phone, then it's time to take a look at the map to see just how far away from help you are. First try to be as certain as possible where you are. GPS coordinates are perfect to plot on your map, but without them you need to be able to read your map and use your compass. Try to get as high as possible to be able to see as much of the terrain around you as you can to identify your location, landmarks, and possible escape routes.

Cold weather is dangerous if you are not prepared for it. It is vital that the body's core temperature is protected, otherwise you face the very real risk of becoming hypothermic and suffering from exposure. The first signs are quite obvious – numbness in the fingers and toes, deep uncontrollable muscular shivering, and stiffness. The second stage of hypothermia might not be so obvious to the sufferer as it involves disorientation and confusion, followed by physical clumsiness and failing coordination. Wind chill can cause you to lose heat extremely quickly, even more so in wet conditions, so wearing appropriate clothing is an essential first line of defence if your route is taking you somewhere cold.

Layering your clothing and sealing gaps are the most effective ways of insulating yourself. Two or three thin layers will always be more effective at keeping you warm than one thick layer. Try to avoid natural fibres as these

↑ Protection from the elements should be your first priority
📷 Touratech

will absorb body moisture which increases the chilling effect as it evaporates. It's better to use clothing made from 'technical' or wicking fabrics which allow the body to breathe without becoming damp. Most overland motorcycling suits are equipped with a removable thermal inner. In extremes of temperature or rainfall, consider also using a one-piece oversuit. Whilst being bulky, the one-piece suit has the advantage of giving wind and rain protection and minimises heat losses or leakage between jacket and trousers.

Fingers and toes will always be the first part of the body to get cold, so take precautions to protect them from the cold.

For all the reasons given above, cold is a quiet killer, so if you find yourself in trouble, then shelter must be an absolute priority. If you have a tent or bivouac, it must be placed as much out of the wind as possible. Using the bike as a windbreak can help. Energy should be conserved wherever possible as you need a lot of it to stay warm.

Use your sleeping bag effectively, and provide as much insulation between you and the ground as possible by using your sleeping mat, foliage or thin branches to act as a barrier. In extreme conditions place spare clothing under your sleeping bag. When inside your bag you should wear your thin base layer underwear,

supplemented if necessary by the thermal liners of your suit. Be careful not to overheat, however, as this can cause high levels of condensation inside the sleeping bag which will dampen the filling and make it less efficient. By day a fire is a good way of keeping warm, as well as attracting attention with smoke.

Having a few key items can make the difference between life and death. Also, never forget that your mindset and your ability to remain calm and not panic are arguably your most important survival tools. A survival kit should consist of:

- Water
- Water filter and purification tablets
- Food
- Emergency blanket
- Torch
- Sharp knife
- Compass
- Map
- Pen or pencil
- Lighter or matches
- Heavy-duty plastic bag
- Wire
- Basic first aid kit
- Personal medication

First aid

Whether you're travelling alone or with a companion, it is wise to take with you at the very least a basic first aid kit and to have a reasonable knowledge of first aid. Any incident, with perhaps the exception of the most trivial, should be treated with a degree of seriousness to prevent it escalating. Even the toughest of adventurers can fall foul of an infection caused by a wound being left untreated or getting dirty.

It is vital that if you ensure a sufficient supply of any prescription medicines you require – don't rely on being able to top-up en route. There are a few basic items that are essential for a traveller's first aid kit, but be warned – it's easy to go overboard and end up taking far more than you'll ever actually need.

The first step is to identify and assess the problem. Are you able to administer aid, or are you likely to compound matters? With an injury like a sprained ankle, you need to think twice about what to do. Can the victim still walk or bear weight? If so, it's probably better to proceed with caution and seek help at the next available stop. A risk attached to this type of injury is swelling – it might not be apparent at first as your boot tends to support the injury site. Remove the boot, however, and the ankle will swell making it impossible to get the boot back on, and there will be no more riding until the swelling subsides.

It's also quite common to twist a knee, easily done as it's instinctive to put a leg out if you feel unstable on the bike. Again, if you can still walk or bear weight it is wise to give extra support by strapping with a compression or elastic bandage, but take special care as a second twist to an already compromised knee is not only excruciatingly painful but carries the risk of permanent damage.

Fractures are harder to deal with in the field and shouldn't really be touched unless you know what you are doing, or have no choice. In the case of a leg fracture, try to immobilise the limb by taping or strapping it to the other 'good' leg. If the fracture is obviously displaced, leave it and go for help. Similar techniques can be used for arm or collarbone fractures, or shoulder dislocation, by using a classic shoulder sling to support the arm, and if necessary bandage or tape it to the torso.

If the injured party is capable of riding pillion and the terrain isn't too rough, then go straight to the nearest settlement for help. Otherwise, make the injured party as comfortable as possible while you go to find assistance. It's important to appreciate that even a small injury, particularly to the hands or feet can compromise your ability to control the motorcycle correctly.

→ A well thought-out first aid kit can literally be a lifesaver

📷 Lifesystems

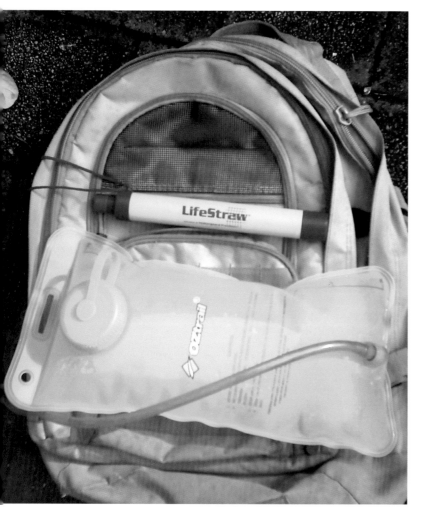

In terms of illness, without doubt the most likely problem you will encounter will be gastric. It is very easy to pick up a stomach bug from badly prepared food or contaminated water. The effects can sometimes be almost immediate, but will usually show anywhere between four to eight hours after consumption. The resulting vomiting and diarrhoea can be particularly unpleasant, and both are remarkably efficient dehydrators. It is vital that you firstly address the danger of dehydration, but drinking purified plain water may not be sufficient as you will rapidly be losing minerals and salts.

Dioralyte is a powdered oral rehydration product available from pharmacies, consisting of various electrolytic salts and glucose which, when added to water, increase the rate at which it can be absorbed into the body. Energy drinks help, as does Coca Cola, but they need to be stirred to remove the fizz before drinking. The high sugar content gives a fast energy boost, and very often this will 'stay down' when other liquids won't. In extreme cases, and in the absence of any of the products mentioned above, a half teaspoon of salt and four to five of sugar mixed in a pint of clean water will be an effective and reasonably palatable substitute.

Don't underestimate the effects of dehydration – the body's coping mechanisms begin to fail as the level of dehydration increases and, with severe dehydration, confusion and weakness will occur as the brain and other body organs receive less blood. This in turn will have a significant impact on your riding, and your ability to concentrate and control the motorcycle.

↑A personal filtration unit is a useful supplement to your hydration system
📷 Andrew Smith

Cuts and lacerations are relatively uncommon motorcycling injuries as we are normally protected by the type of clothing we wear. However, basic first aid rules still apply. Wound cleanliness is important as infection is always a danger. Measures should be taken to clean the wound area if possible, or at the very least prevent further contamination of the wound. Cooled boiled water, to which a small amount of salt has been added, makes an effective cleansing solution and is also mildly antiseptic.

If a wound bleeds profusely, then firm pressure, using a clean dressing applied to the area, will very often staunch the flow of blood, allowing further treatment to be administered. In any case it is imperative that the wound is closed, and in the absence of the medical skills required to stitch or suture a wound, dressing tape can be used to hold a cut or tear together. Any injury of this nature will require prompt medical attention at the earliest possible opportunity.

Medical Kit Essentials
- Syringe and needles
- Painkillers
- Anti-inflammatory tablets
- Anesthetic cream
- Eye bath and drops
- Diarrhoea remedy
- Rehydration sachets
- Broad-spectrum antibiotic
- Antiseptic liquid and/or wipes
- Sterile field gloves
- Scissors and tweezers
- Suture kit
- Micropore tape
- Cohesive support bandages
- Compression swabs
- Sanitary tampons
- Variety of fabric plasters

Group riding and dynamics

An important choice before you head off on an adventure is whether to ride alone, with a friend, or as part of a larger group, as it has implications on a number of fronts. If you've had some overland experience, then a solo trip can be considered, but if you are new to adventure motorcycling, then joining a larger party in the form of a group of friends, or even a commercially operated trip, may be the best way of achieving your goal.

if you get into any difficulty, mechanical or otherwise, you will either have to fix it yourself or rely on the assistance of passers by. Drop your bike over in soft sand and you'll soon be wishing you had someone with you to help! There is great satisfaction in a solo achievement, though you will not have anyone to share both the good and bad memories of the trip. You will also have to deal with things directly and will be forced to interact with the local population far more to get things done.

Going Solo

Going solo certainly offers maximum flexibility – you can follow your own route, stop when you want to, and set a riding pace that you feel comfortable with. The downside is that you are more vulnerable when travelling solo, and

Two Up

Travelling with a friend who shares the same goals and expectations can be hugely rewarding. That said, some of the world's best known expeditions and adventure travels have been undone, or at least unhinged, by differing

⬇ Riding solo affords you maximum flexibility
📷 Touratech

↓ Catch me if you can…!

📷 Thorvaldur Orn Kristmundsson

personalities and characters, so it's important to know the person you're travelling with, understand their expectations and concerns (at the same time sharing your own), and even go so far as to have a plan in your mind as to how to deal with the situation if it all goes horribly wrong and you decide to part company from one another midway through the ride. In these circumstances, always carefully consider the merits of splitting up, the risks involved and the importance of the friendship before making any decision. Riding pillion is an option but this has some serious implications – the added weight of a passenger makes the bike harder to control, particularly over rough terrain or very soft sand. The other downside is that storage space is constrained, and carrying gear for two people means your overall load will increase still further.

Groups

Even with the best intentions, it is unlikely that you will be able to establish a large group of people all willing to commit to the same objective, budget, and time frame. Initial enthusiasm soon disappears in some as the real implications sink in, and you are more likely to end up with a much smaller group than initially planned. If you can successfully get a group together, this has a number of advantages:

■ It offers a level of security – there is safety in numbers, and with that comes an element of responsibility for one another.

■ There is likely to be a broad set of skills – some in the group may be more technically minded, while others may be good at navigating, first aid, or planning.

It's a great way to build your experience and prepare for a solo trip.
One is able to share experiences, duties, and decision making.

On the downside, group travel generally means:

One doesn't get to interact with locals as much.
There is likely to be limited flexibility in the route, with different interests across the group.
There may be pressure to meet set objectives.
There may be an uncomfortable group dynamic and personality clashes amongst group members.

Sometimes the smallest thing can trigger a reaction in people, particularly if you are thrust into a Third World environment where there may be limited communications, little or inaccurate information from which to make decisions, climate extremes, disinterested civil servants, and a language barrier to deal with. Bearing in mind the risks associated with each potential scenario, it is vital to discuss this in the planning stages, and to formulate strategies for dealing with them.

A more structured trip offers several key points worth considering, especially if you are new to adventure motorcycling, including:

Fewer unknowns (such as costs), and more structure.
An opportunity to travel with and meet like-minded people, perhaps even make friends for future trips.
The benefit of local knowledge and the chance to explore less well-known routes.

The Making of *Adventure Riding Techniques*

Thorvaldur working his magic in Iceland
📷 Robert Wicks

Despite the availability of a wealth of adventure motorcycling photography, it was always going to be difficult to find sufficient step-by-step imagery to fully illustrate a book of this nature. To overcome this problem the authors travelled to Iceland and teamed up with the country's leading adventure motorcycle tour company, the appropriately named Biking Viking.

'I had travelled around Iceland before but only in a 4x4 vehicle and always felt this would be one of the best places in the world for off-road riding,' explains author Robert Wicks. Covering some 103,000km², Iceland offered some of the most diverse geography and was ideally suited as the backdrop for the photography.

The authors enlisted the help of Simon Pavey, one of the United Kingdom's leading off-road riders and seven-times Dakar Rally participant. 'I'd heard the riding in Iceland was good, but I never expected such breathtaking scenery and such a diverse environment with so many different types of terrain,' says Simon who runs BMW's off-road skills training school in Wales.

'Having consistency in the images we had to work with was key to the layout of the book, and a lot of planning went into the various techniques we had to photograph. With their expert knowledge of the country, the team at Biking Viking ensured we got all we needed,' says co-author Greg Baker.

Index

The Biking Vikings

Eythor Orlygsson - A partner in Biking Viking, he's an experienced off-road rider whose expert mechanical skills are often put to the test on the more difficult highland tours. Eythor has been to every corner of Iceland, but he broke his leg in a bike accident just days before the trip and opted to drive the support vehicle.

Ingolfur Stefansson - A partner in Biking Viking, who also runs the official Land Rover 4x4 adventure company franchise in Iceland and knows the country like the back of his hand. He cooks the best lamb in Iceland and has a unique ability to pose.

Njall Gunnlaugsson - The founder of Biking Viking who has been riding motorcycles for 25 years. He is a certified instructor and has written the history of motorcycling in Iceland.

Hjortur L. Jonsson - The 'old man' of the group, who leads from the front and is deceptively quick across any type of terrain. This man knew exactly where to find every scenario we had to shoot. He had some of the funniest motorcycle stories to tell and his leather riding cap had us laughing for hours.

Thorgeir Olason - Our second guide and the 'quiet man' of the group. He is an extremely talented rider and could comfortably ride at the highest level.

Thorvaldur Orn Kristmundsson - This was the man behind the lens in Iceland and he produced most of the stunning imagery for the book.

The group spent a week together in Iceland in August 2008, taking the photographs and researching the book.

Listings

Books

Adventure Motorcycling by Robert Wicks, published by Haynes (ISBN 9781844254354), offers insight into all aspects of long-distance adventure riding with a specific section on riding techniques, terrain, and training schools.

Chasing Dakar by Jonathan Edwards and Scot Harden (ISBN 0978709403), offers practical advice about off-road riding, with a specific focus on preparing for the Dakar Rally.

Adventure Motorcycling Handbook by Chris Scott, published by Trailblazer Publications (ISBN 1873756372), contains a short section dedicated to off-road riding techniques.

Riding the World by Gregory Frazier, published in 2005 by Bowtie Press (ISBN 1931993246), touches on the subject of techniques.

Pro Motocross and Off-road Riding Techniques by Donnie Bales, published by Motorbooks International (ISBN 0760318026).

Motocross and Off-Road Training Handbook by Mark Thompson, published by Motorbooks International (ISBN 0760321132).

Motocross Fitness: The Ultimate Home Training Guide for Motocross Athletes by Rodney Womack.

Going the Extra Mile by Ron Ayres published in 2002 by White Horse Press (ISBN 1884313396), covers insider tips for long-distance motorcycling.

DVDs

Miles Ahead – endurance and adventure against the clock
The Ride – Alaska to Patagonia
Long Way Round
Long Way Down
Riding South America – Peru and Patagonia
Mondo Enduro
Terra Circa
Moto Syberia

Websites

www.acerbis.it
www.adventuremotorcycle.org
www.adventure-motorcycling.com
www.advrider.com
www.berndtesch.de
www.camelbak.com
www.dainese.com
www.dualsportnews.com
www.dualsportmagazine.com
www.expertgps.com
www.flamesonmytank.co.za
www.globalenduro.com
www.globebusters.com
www.globeriders.com
www.happy-trail.com
www.harden-offroad.com
www.haynes.co.uk
www.hein-gericke.com
www.horizonsunlimited.com
www.josef-pichler.at
www.kriega.com
www.kuduexpeditions.com
www.lifesystems.co.uk
www.metalmule.com
www.motionpro.com
www.motoaventures.com
www.nippynormans.com
www.offroadskills.com
www.ortlieb.com
www.overland-solutions.com
www.pac-safe.com
www.pelican.com
www.rawhyde-offroad.com
www.rukka.com
www.touratech.com
www.transamtrail.com
www.traveldri-plus.co.uk
www.tukutuku.de
www.whitehorsepress.com
www.worldofbmw.com
www.wunderlich.de
www.zyro.co.uk

To contact the authors, please e-mail:
adventuremotorcycling@gmail.com